EZ.

MARATHON

MARATHON

The Story of Civilizations
on Collision Course

Alan Lloyd

READERS UNION
Group of Book Clubs
Newton Abbot 1975

First published by Souvenir Press

This edition was produced in 1975 for sale to its members
only by the proprietors, Readers Union Limited,
PO Box 6, Newton Abbot, Devon, TQ12 2DW.
Full details of membership will gladly be sent on request

Reproduced and printed in Great Britain
by Redwood Burn Limited
Trowbridge & Esher for Readers Union

Dedicated to the legion of leisure readers who, like myself, remain rapt and wide-eyed in a permanent inaugural term of history—with special affection for Ann, Judy, Alan, Ron, and their felicitous contribution to the younger generation

As on the morn to distant Glory
dear,
When Marathon became a
magic word—
          —Byron, *Childe Harold*

Contents

PART FOUR: A Time for Heroes

Part 1
Concerning Little States

> For we are lovers of the beauti-
> ful, yet simple in our tastes, and
> we cultivate the mind without
> loss of manliness.
> —Thucydides

One day when that sad, brilliant, restless and incorrigible giant called Western Civilization was very young—a mere infant in the sunny cradle of the Balkan Peninsula—a great emperor of the East sent his warriors to claim it and baptize it in the style of his regime: despotism.

Whereupon the men of the infant civilization, more particularly of Athens, its brightest gem, took swords and armor, bade farewell to their women and marched to face the invaders where the blue Aegean touched the soil of ancient Greece. Many of the women, filled with anxiety, gathered flowers and carried them to the threshold of their homes where the guardian Herm kept vigil, his carved head and erect stone phallus boding luck and fertility. Here, placing wreaths of anemones and other blooms on the sacred image, the wives of Athens offered prayers for the safe return of husbands, sons and lovers.

Since Athens was small and the despot's warriors numerous, the first thing the men needed, after the blessing of their gods, was reinforcement. This raised a problem. Because the Greeks lived in tight little city-states, isolated from their neighbors by seas and mountains, they were obliged to cover long distances to seek one another's help.

Accordingly, when the citizens of Athens knew that the emperor's army was coming, they dispatched a trained long-distance runner west to the Corinthian isthmus, then south across the craggy ranges of the Peloponnesus, to request aid of the citizens of Sparta, about a hundred and fifty miles away. The name of the runner was Philippides, or, as some maintain, Pheidippides; the former will be used in these pages.

Twenty-five centuries later, it would be absurd to pretend an intimate knowledge of Philippides and his contemporaries. Rather, their remoteness keeps the Greeks of old fresh for the modern reader. Of all people, they, who relished truth unadorned, would have despised the sham familiarity heaped on too many of historic fame. What *can* be said about Philippides, not only on the evidence of the story which will unfold but on the knowledge that the Greeks produced fine athletes as readily as fine minds, is that he must have been a man of exceptional stamina. The Athenians might have sent a horseman to Sparta. That instead they chose a runner tells something of the rigors of the terrain and more of the faith they placed in human performance.

Hellenic art, the art of the ancient Greeks, or Hellenes, abounds in subjects of athletic prowess. In picturing Philippides, it is worth contemplating a vivid illustration which has survived of a foot race in the Panathenaic games, a festival of sport held every four years in the city. It is a dynamic portrait of racing men. Lean, slim of waist and splendidly muscled, some wearing trim beards, the naked contestants are athletes of superb physique. Philippides, as an exponent of the dolichos, or long foot race, may well have made a name for himself in these games or the Olympics, held on the banks of the Alpheus in the western Peloponnesus.

Now, as crisis gripped Athens, the runner loped west with the steady, relaxed gait of the distance specialist, pacing himself for the grueling miles to Sparta.

The news Philippides carried was ominous for much of Greece. Bent on subjugating Athens, the armada of Darius, emperor of Persia, was off the east coast. Nobody underrated the emperor—lord of the Orient, as his people had it, the king of kings, with dominion "over this earth afar and its subjects of many tongues."

The Persian empire was the overwhelming power of that ancient world. Its constituents reached from the Bosporus to the Punjab, from Egypt to Georgia in Caucasia, embracing and overflowing the best part of what maps today term the Middle East. Across these vast tracts, Darius could summon fierce highlanders from Afghanistan and Hyrcania, the "Wolf's Land" of old Persia; wild horsemen from the steppes of Khurasan, north of the Hindu Kush; black archers from Ethiopia; imperial swordsmen from his barracks at Pasargadae and Persepolis; warriors of diverse description from the lands of the empire's great rivers, the Indus, Oxus, Nile, Euphrates and the Tigris. Beside the Persian colossus, the states of Greece were Lilliputian.

Darius, to be fair, was no ogre. As despots go, he was not a bad one. A man of some honor and scruple, a builder rather than a destroyer, he slaughtered only those who persisted in thwarting him. It is, after all, one of the awkward facts of life for a well-meaning despot that once he tolerates being thwarted his potency vanishes.

For those under his sprawling rule, life probably was better, on the whole, than for those beyond it, where most people still dwelt in primitive insecurity. Nevertheless, life under Darius meant obeying the whims of the emperor or those to whom he allowed authority in his name. There was no argument. There were no politics as they are now understood in the regime—any more than there had been politics under Rameses or Nebuchadnezzar. There were no public affairs in the empire, only the private affairs of the sovereign and his privileged ruling class. There was no consultation with the people or even a substantial group of them. Government was simply a matter of the wishes and power of the ruler.

In itself, the situation affronted few under Darius, for the notion of personal liberties did not become widespread until later times, and what those in the empire had not known they could not miss. It did, however, affront the Greeks—not all of them, since no society is of wholly like mind and interests, but a sufficient number by the fifth century B.C. to cause irritation on the western fringe of the empire. It affronted them because, though geographically scattered and otherwise divided, the Greeks shared some remarkably persistent attributes, not least an avid taste for inquiry, disputation and discovery. They liked to find out about life. They liked adventuring, not only outwardly in the sense that drove their traders to the furthermost reaches of the Mediterranean, but also inwardly in the sense that they were psychologists, explorers of their own minds. And one of their discoveries, the more appealing to many since it harnessed philosophy to practical advantage—and the Greeks were, above all things, realists—happened to be politics.

By the time Darius was established as the absolute ruler of the empire, the Greeks had recognized, and begun to provide for, the fact that public or common interest had a part to play in government. This might have had little impact on their lives, let alone on the world at large, if they had been careless in the application of their theories and had been a race with big ideas yet small talent for the crafts through which they must be realized. But they were not. On the contrary, the Greeks did most things exceedingly well. They expected high standards. When the Greeks went to a play, they expected a fine play. When they bought pots for their kitchens, they expected to buy fine pots. Doubtless, they were often disappointed. But when people expect the best, average standards tend to be fairly good.

Admittedly, such people can be tiresome to those who may wish, with equal right, to get by on what will suffice. In the end, whether or not the strivings and innovations of Western society are considered to have made for a richer life than, say, the less demanding rhythms of some still-primitive jungle tribe is a matter of personal temperament. What cannot be denied is that the urge to excel is a prerequisite of what is called progress, and that those endowed with it retain our attention and excitement more readily than those of languishing standards.

The creations of ancient Greece proved incredibly durable. Tens of hundreds of years after Hellenic society passed away, students would still be making standard use of a textbook by a Greek geometrician, a scientific discourse by a Greek grammarian and an ethical treatise by a Greek doctor—these in the most changeable field of scholarship, science. In other regions of intellectual activity, the fruits of Greek endeavor seem virtually imperishable. For some reason which defies explanation, the people of those small Balkan and Aegean communities, so similar in background to the "barbarians" they affected to despise, were stimulated to such intensity by certain concepts —truth, beauty, freedom, excellence—that they obtained a concentration of achievement unrivaled in history.

Consider that in a single century one Greek city, no larger than a rural market town of modern times, was home to a greater wealth of genius than many nations can boast in their whole existence. Aeschylus, the founder of drama; the philosopher Anaxagorus; Aristophanes, the great comic dramatist; the playwright Euripides; Herodotus, "the father of history"; Hippocrates, "the father of medicine"; the orator Isocrates; Phidias, one of the world's outstanding sculptors; Pindar, the lyric poet; Plato, preeminent philosopher of the West; Protagoras, philosopher and grammarian; the sublime tragic poet Sophocles; the historian Thucydides. All, and more, were familiar figures on the streets of fifth-century Athens—the century of Marathon.

Greek thought, assimilated and spread by the Romans, neglected in the Dark Ages, and hailed anew in the Renaissance, was to lead Western society to the forefront of world affairs, then return and free the Orient itself from despotism and stagnation. But that was all far ahead. By the beginning of the fifth century, the Greeks were only tickling the flank of their huge eastern neighbor.

It so happened that Athens, no less opportunist than many a bright prospect, had sent aid to the rebel colony of Ionia, an ancient province on the Aegean coast of Asia Minor—it lay between the Smyrna Gulf and the Gulf of Kerme—which was struggling to gain independence from the Persian empire. It was this brash impertinence, as Darius saw it, which had drawn his attention to Athens and unleashed his vengeance.

The Persian armada descended on the mainland near the village of Marathon, twenty-two miles from the city. The imperial army had two possible routes to its objective: it could cross the hills which stretched south from Mount Parnes to Mount Hymettus, screening the city from Marathon, or it could detour Hymettus to the south, beside the Saronic Gulf. With the hills left behind, the little city—magical to the Persians, who had nothing to compare with it—would lie before the invaders vulnerable as a lark's nest on the gently sloping Attic plain.

From the west, Philippides could look back from his path on the same scene. There, plainly signed by the crown of Lycabettus, were the temples and statues, the market and assembly place, the honeycombed Hill of Nymphs, the springs, the terraces, the academies, the courts of art and entertainment, the indelible Acropolis. It was the nest from which soared the Greek spirit on free wings.

But all the spirit in the world, by itself, could not stop the Persian army, a host of awesome size and reputation which had marched the Asiatic unbeaten. It would take stout men, well armed, to save Athens from the despot, and she could raise from her able-bodied freemen just nine thousand.

Prelude 2

The curtain of history, it has been said, ascends on a night sky in which, here and there, a rare star feebly twinkles. This is not to say that such stars, the stars of the earliest cultivated societies, were really feeble; it is simply that sheer distance has diminished their power for us.

From the moment people banded in groups for company and safety, countless societies have formed, divided and perished. They have been doing so for hundreds of thousands of years; yet, to our knowledge, those that have created civilizations can be counted on the fingers, with perhaps a toe or two added, of a single man. For most of his long and anxious existence, *Homo sapiens* was too busy surviving to think about much more than his skin and his stomach. And without time to think, he could not refine, could not add style to his way of life.

It was ages before man found a spot in which to sit and meditate. When, at last, a few people got around to it, they did so pretty much in the places we might expect. It was least likely where the natural elements increased human hardship: in tropical forests, in deserts, in regions of frost and ice. It was most likely to occur where a combination of warmth and provident waters made for comfort and fertile lands, the saving of man's energies. The earliest stars of civilization shine on calm rivers in areas where the climate soothes the human breast.

About 4,270 years ago a glimmer of light appeared over the India of the lower Indus, and three centuries later, over the Hwang-ho valley of China. At the same time, stars of a brighter order began to glow above the rivers of Egypt and Mesopotamia, where the first urban civilizations were developing. In

9

the nineteenth century B.C., the Pharaohs of the Twelfth Dynasty rose in brilliance on the Nile, while in Mesopotamia, the Land of Two Rivers at the head of the Persian Gulf, a monument to progress called Babylon was founded. Egypt and Babylon gleamed for their allotted spans.

Time is a stern dispenser of justice. It imposes an inexorable sentence on races or societies which outstrip their less fortunate fellow-men. When wild animals are domesticated, and life is handed them on a plate, they lose some of their survival instincts. So it is when part of the human race comes together as a comfortable elite. At the same time, the survival instincts of its backward neighbors remain sharp.

If a civilization is insular and stays small, it lives with covetous hordes on the doorstep. If it expands, forms an empire, its arteries are stretched and its frontiers weakened, and the hordes break in and tear out its flabby heart. These hordes, the rude enemies of civilized societies, were soon cast as the villains of the ancient world: barbarians, savages, rapist brutes. It is well to be cautious of such labels. Civilizations are articulate, though the records are loaded against folk who cannot answer back.

Today, it is hard to visualize economic conditions at the time of the early civilizations. What now passes for malnutrition must then have been regarded by most as an enviable state of health. In a single poor season, whole tribes were annihilated by starvation. Unsurprisingly, people fought for those lands which promised the best share of the food of life. Migration, and the conflicts which sprang from it, were an inevitable part of human development. A tribe moved from barren lands to more hospitable regions, and if it was stronger than the people already there, they, in turn, migrated to harass those of other lands. Constantly searching for fruitful ground, the human tides surged hungrily to the borders of the civilized areas. And there, it surely seemed to the wanderers, was paradise—lands where fat beasts grazed, ripening corn waved, and the vales were rich in milk and honey.

Among the great migratory invasions of the ancient East, one in particular stands out in the furthermost reaches of this saga. No such story has a definite starting point, but the people now known as the Indo-Europeans may serve as a convenient beginning, if only because their own beginnings are so vague. Some scholars believe they arose from the regions of Austria and Hungary; others, that they came from central Asia. They were probably not of common racial stock, but they did speak languages fashioned from a single tongue, and they were formidable warriors.

In their migrations, the Indo-Europeans traveled with unusual speed. They had horses. Indeed, they may have been the first people to ride horseback. They also had a convincing form of passport in the heavy battle-axes they cast in bronze. By the end of the third millennium B.C., these shaggy, adventurous nomads had ranged Asia Minor and probed the Balkan Peninsula to the Gulf of Corinth.

The flurry of further migration they set up around them was to be important to the evolution of both the Persian empire and ancient Greece. It foreshadowed, too, the end of Egypt's power and brilliance.

Meanwhile, surrounded by the kindly moat of the eastern Mediterranean, a colorful new civilization had flowered in Crete, between cultivated Egypt and a still uncultured Greece. The outstanding difference between the Cretans and other advanced people of the period was that, being islanders, they were a seafaring race. The protection of the sea gave them time to sit and make things; their skill as sailors enabled them to bear their wares to distant parts.

Extraordinarily enough, Cretan civilization—its later stages are also known as Minoan, after a legendary king, Minos—was not discovered for the modern world until well into our own century, when archaeologists uncovered the remains of a great palace on the island, at Knossos, a mile or so south of present-day Candia.

Further discoveries confirmed that the ancient Cretans were

far ahead of other Mediterranean races (with the exception of the Egyptians) as architects, draftsmen and builders. They also excelled as goldsmiths and engravers, and as makers of vividly colored ceramics.

Not only at Knossos but at Mallia, Phaestus and other towns the ruling families built massive residences to proclaim their fortunes and house their treasure, chapels, archives, provisions and spices. In one aspect, however, they lacked foresight. So confident were the Cretan monarchs in their sea power that fortifications were considered unnecessary.

Their ships maintained trade with Egypt, carried colonists to various parts of the Aegean, and eventually established Cretan communities on the Greek mainland. At Mycenae and Tiryns, both on the Argive plain between the gulfs of Argos and Corinth, they watched over the route from Crete to central Greece.

At this point, a significant union of cultures arises, a form of marriage not uncommon in history and which often produces the stuff of memorable drama. It is a marriage, as it were, between a lady of refined caste, Cretan culture, and an ambitious partner of coarser breeding, the warlike Achaean. The Achaeans came from Thessaly, north of the Pinthos Range, before moving into southern Greece. Because Mycenae became the symbol of its influence, the result of the union is known as Mycenaean Greece.

Mycenaean culture, blending Cretan artistry with Achaean utility and aggression, is preserved in a sumptuous bounty of gold and silver artifacts depicting, with striking enthusiasm, scenes of hunting and warfare. In Mycenaean Greece, the Cretan palace became a stronghold, a purposeful Bronze Age castle in which warrior princes, bedecked with daggers and amulets set with precious metals, drank wine from golden goblets before sallying forth to engage their foes.

Among the first to suffer was Crete itself, sea power no longer being an assurance against enemies who had received nautical skills in a rich marriage dowry. The downfall of Knossos, about 1500 B.C., betokened the close of civilization in the island.

From there the Achaeans roved to Rhodes and Cyprus, prowled the Cyclades and sailed north to the Hellespont. Ancient Greece was poor in productive land, as it is today—less than a quarter of the country is cultivable—and the rulers in the south were always on the lookout for supplies abroad. An especially promising field was the shores of the Euxine, but getting there meant a passage through the narrow waters of the Hellespont, which joins the Aegean to the Black Sea. And the gates of the Hellespont were commanded by the rulers of Troy, in the far northwest of Asia Minor, the land known to the Greeks as Phrygia.

The Trojan War, though by far the most celebrated feat of Achaean arms under the leadership of Mycenae, owes its fame more to myth than to scientific data.

In Greek legend, King Priam of Troy ruled all that is bounded by "Lesbos, Phrygia and the Hellespont." Priam had fifty sons, so the tale goes, including Paris, whose distinctions included that of being the first reported judge of a beauty contest. It was the dubious privilege of Paris to select the most desirable of three goddesses, Athena, Hera and Aphrodite, creatures of a divine loveliness not unmatched by a somewhat down-to-earth bitchiness.

When Aphrodite was awarded the accolade, Athena and Hera promised that Troy should suffer for their misuse. The winner, on the other hand, granted Paris the love of the fairest woman living. So it came to pass that Paris, visiting Greece, won the favor of a beautiful heiress, Helen, whom he carried away to Troy. The curse of Athena and Hera was already implicit, for Helen was married to an Achaean prince.

To recover Helen and avenge the insult, the Achaeans attacked Troy under King Agamemnon of Mycenae. But the walls of Troy were too strong for them. For ten years they besieged the city without success, until they finally resorted to their famed ruse. Building a huge wooden horse, the Greeks concealed a squad of their heroes in its belly, then pretended to retire from Troy, leaving the horse behind. Overjoyed by the departure of their enemies, the Trojans dragged the horse within their walls before proceeding to celebrate. The hidden heroes awaited nightfall, crept from their refuge and opened the city gates to their comrades. At last Troy was taken.

All of which is a very fanciful explanation of how the Achaeans came to overthrow the Trojans, as they undoubtedly did. Yet the story is relevant, for while Achaean reality is important, if short-lived—the Achaeans were soon overwhelmed by the Dorians, an even ruder people, and Greece consigned again to darkness—its fanciful counterpart, the Heroic Age portrayed in Greek myth, is not only more important but still alive.

To Philippides the runner, and his comrades of a later day, Mycenaean Greece was the golden era of their heritage, an epoch of champions, recalled through the mist of poetic inventiveness rather as we hark back ourselves to the age of King Arthur and the knights of our fabled past. The inspiration which fired them must be sought in a fairy tale.

The Myth 3

No athlete relies more on sheer determination than the marathon runner, the long-distance specialist. His is the epic test, the ordeal that destroys wind and muscle. When his legs become leaden, his eyes glazed, his lungs bladders of pain within burning ribs, mind alone sustains him in his pursuit. As Philippides struggled west through the harsh mountain passes, his journey increasingly became a trial of character.

Today's athletes are very conscious of mental attitudes, of psychological barriers. Greek athletes, in their own way, recognized the same power of mind over physique. By placing faith in their gods and emulating their heroes they sought to gain extra performance. Call it character, spirit, or what you will, it was this sense of heroic destiny which lifted Philippides on the tortuous path to Sparta as surely as it inspired Athens to defy the "invincible" Persian host. Among the people of their time, the Greeks had an exceptional mentality, and the key to it lies in the magic world of Greek myth.

Since the period the legends of the Heroic Age first began to crystallize, the Hellenes looked to the tellers of *mythoi*, or tales from the past, to fashion noble models in which they could seek themselves. They found encouragement for their own endeavors in the glorious exploits recalled by the poets and singers. The quickening of ideals by stories of example is a well-recognized preparation for human achievement. Plato had no doubt of this. In the ideal society of his *Republic*, the relating of myths came before factual or rational teaching on the literary curriculum.

Philippides, as any other Greek of his own day, would have encountered myth in one form or another at every turn of life.

As a child, he would have imbibed the mythical tradition at the family hearth in gripping stories of marvel and adventure, many of which survive in the great sagas of the Trojan cycle, the *Odyssey* and the *Iliad*. Eyes bright, mouths agape, Athenian children would be transported from the knees of their parents to the heights of Olympus, the home of fantastic and fetchingly capricious gods. From here they might look down on mortal heroes: watch Priam's son Hector battle with the redoubtable Achilles; follow Odysseus into the city of the Phaeacians; sail with Jason in search of the Golden Fleece. Or they might venture abroad with the gods themselves: ride with Phaëthon behind the winged horses of the sun chariot, float to earth in a cloud with the goddess Hera to chastise her husband's lover, Io, or sigh with Europa as Zeus charmed her in the form of a white bull.

As the audience grew older the significance of myth increased. What the child absorbed in exciting but unpolished fable the youth rediscovered in art and poetry; what the youth admired in pure form the adult digested at the theater, its relevance updated and stressed by the immediacy of drama.

For the Greek dramatist, the characters of legend were hugely rewarding because they were already so real to the audience. And because the Greek mind was intrigued by the laws of human conduct—by why people were as they were—the characters of Greek drama were real in a deep and universal sense. The Athenian theatergoer, on his hard bench, would have had no time for the two-dimensional heroes of lesser folklore, for the shining perfection of St. George of England or the whiter-than-white cowboy knight of the Wild West.

The Greeks realized that drama lay not only in the conflict between human beings, but in the conflict which exists in each person. For them, Prometheus, the legendary character portrayed by Aeschylus as a champion of the weak and a lover of humanity, was the more real for being shown also as overconfident in his own powers and arrogant toward the gods. Achilles, essentially noble and honorable, was the more real for his outbursts of intolerance against those who offended his sense of propriety. Again, King Oedipus, whose brilliant mind could see through all problems, was convincingly blind to his own responsibility for the disaster which befell his subjects.

The Greeks admired their heroes no less for possessing human weaknesses. Indeed, without them no hero would have been accepted as credible.

Nor were the gods of fable unerring. For all their supernatural powers, they existed in a realm of entirely natural desires and jealousies, bounded in their relationships by the type of pecking order modern sociologists have discerned as a feature of societies at all levels. Deities of both sexes, unblushing in their partiality for mortal favorites, used their divine powers not only to support those they patronized, but to gain what they desired from them. Zeus, the greatest of all gods in Greek myth, was a confirmed seducer of mortal damsels, whose delights he sought in many guises.

Though the Greeks selected what they chose to admire in the Heroic Age, they accepted its overall naturalness with a perhaps enviable lack of many of the guilts, suppressions and frustrations which impinged on a later age.

No one could pretend that the Achaeans were a model people in any modern sense. They were rough, aggressive, cruel and acquisitive, but as their thoughtful descendants realized, such attributes coexist in all people with more exciting qualities: bravery, humor, generosity, tenderness.

The Achaeans lived, even at the upper levels of society portrayed in Greek myth, a hard life of primitive amenities. Yet while they flourished, it did allow them freedoms denied by the complex social restrictions of our own day. In a way, as a source of inspiration to the Greece to come, their value was enhanced by this lack of inhibition, this candidness.

In particular, the relationship between the sexes was free of much of the bitterness and misogynism that came later with the spread of a sex-abhorring ethic—a phenomenon that has persisted in many quarters until present times, and would have seemed quite bizarre to the ancient Greeks.

Intelligent, enterprising, gay, sensuous and self-assured, the women of the Heroic Age not infrequently come across as precisely the kind of complete and rather exceptional females the twentieth century A.D. regards as "emancipated."

Marriage appears to have involved a refreshing degree of understanding and tolerance, for though monogamy was the custom, myth acknowledges a good deal of freedom among both sexes, attaching no stigma to extramarital connections. Of course, there was rivalry and jealousy. Strong currents have never made smooth water.

The exasperation of Zeus's wife, Hera, queen of the gods, at her husband's persistent resort to the daughters of mortals and demigods is amusingly recounted in the legends, but there was no enduring grudge between them. The Greeks considered it natural that Zeus should pay court to lovely girls, such as Europa and Io, just as they regarded it natural that the goddess Thetis should be the lover of King Peleus, or Aphrodite the lover of a handsome prince.

In the exclusively mortal domain, it was much the same. Penelope, wife of Odysseus, did not hold her husband's lovers, Circe and Calypso, against him; nor did Helen suffer any loss of reputation for making the most of her stay in Troy. Having left a husband in Greece, she not only married Paris but, on his death, wed his brother, Deïphobus. Finally, when Troy fell, she returned to Greece and lived again as the respected wife of her original spouse. Absence might make the heart grow fonder, but it was not held to necessitate abstinence.

That woman needed man, as man woman, was considered self-evident, and arrangements were made to suit the need at convenience. This is not to say that love was taken lightly. On the contrary, it was seen as a powerful and poetic force. Under its influence, a mighty god could become obsessed by a girl he found minding her father's flock on a hillside. And if this was lust, its corollary was tenderness. When Achilles raided Lyrnessus in the course of the Trojan War, he carried off Briseis among his girl captives. It is clear in the *Iliad* that, though Briseis could be regarded crudely as a spoil of war, the two were in love in a devoted sense. When they parted, the girl was miserable, and Achilles was moved to express a distinctly chivalric sentiment: "Does not every decent and right-minded man love and cherish his own woman, as I loved that girl, with all my heart, though she was a captive of my spear?"

Unsurprisingly, the freedom of women, plus the lack of sexual inhibition in Heroic Greece, was attended by a high incidence of birth out of wedlock. At the same time, there was no discredit to unmarried mothers or their offspring. Men of rank were often born out of wedlock. For not a few, it was even an advantage, since the absence of a flesh-and-blood father enabled them to romanticize their parents. The reputation of the gods must have tempted the tongue of many an ambitious and imaginative maiden caught with child after a woodland romp with a sporting nonentity. If she chose to boast of an encounter with an immortal lover, who could disprove her?

One of Achilles' lieutenants, Menesthius, an officer of high repute, was said to be the love-child of a woman and a river god, Spercheus. Another, the noted runner Eudorus, whose mother was a comely dancer, was proclaimed the son of the versatile god Hermes. Both their unmarried mothers afterward became the wives of wealthy men who paid handsomely for them in dowries.

Whether one regards the legendary attitudes as happily innocent or deplorably indulgent—and the Achaeans themselves were something of each at times—the life-style of the gods and heroes provided for Greek consumption a rich study in human behavior, one, moreover, steeped in the presumption of personal liberty. True, not even the gods and lordly heroes of myth were entirely immune from social restriction, but compared with their humbler contemporaries, and certainly anyone in the present age, they had unusual scope to behave as they wished, for good or bad.

Myth, therefore, implanted the idea of liberty deep in the Greek mind. By developing in vivid and haunting images some of the consequences of free choice, it also cultivated a taste for moral reflection, a sense of social responsibility. By the fifth century, Herodotus could make an assertion most of the world would then have found meaningless, but which, twenty-four centuries later, would be acknowledged by the mass of people everywhere. "Liberty and Equality," he wrote, "are brave, spirit-stirring things."

When Philippides set out to run to Sparta, he was not impelled by the will of an overlord to secure the power of some prince or tribal chieftain. Philippides was running in accord with a deep-rooted urge for freedom, for a voice in his own destiny.

By the beginning of the century of Marathon, reason and experience had led the Greeks to intellectual heights beyond the foothills of simple myth. The desire to explain things that had previously been accepted without question was growing fast. As science and philosophy developed, the old stories were seen in a new light. The word "mythical" came to mean legendary in the specific sense. The tales were miraculous, undemonstrable. It was only a short step from undemonstrable to unreal. Yet, earlier generations had accepted myth as historic fact—tales of glory which had survived the Dark Ages to link the emerging Greece with an epic past.

Attitudes move in strange cycles. When Christianity became a social force, it tolerated myth because the legends were assumed to be entirely fictitious, of no more than aesthetic significance. Today, interest has swung back to the factual element, with scholars busily seeking the links between legend and reality: Crete's maritime achievements, the kings of Knossos and Mycenae, the martial exploits of the Achaeans.

Like all good stories, myth is both experience and imagination. In the course of centuries, the historic seed gave rise to oral traditions embellished by the poetic fancy of those who tended and passed on the living plant.

At first, it was minstrels, singing for a livelihood in the courts of noblemen or in the city markets, who proclaimed the wonders of the Heroic Age. Their primitive songs—songs of "praise for the deeds of gods and men," as they were known —were the forerunners of Greek epic poetry, which enhanced myth with a broader vision of life and added a conscious touch of racial pride.

Interestingly enough, the most renowned of the epic poets, Homer, long regarded as the author of the *Odyssey* and the *Iliad*, lived not in Greece but among the settlements of Ionia, possibly Chios. Since his name means hostage, it is possible he was abducted from the Greek mainland in his youth. Certainly, as with many a colonial, his strong feelings of racial identity are evident.

Homer lived, probably, in the ninth century B.C. Soon, other poets, working in the same style, began to set out lengthy epics, the so-called cyclic poems, to extend or supplement the chronology of the Trojan War. Some invented elaborate pedigrees tracing the mythical heroes back to ancient gods and forward to their own noble contemporaries. From their urge to chart and rationalize the past came historiography.

Toward the end of the sixth century, the extraordinary vitality of Greek legend burst forth in a new and dramatic form of poetry, the tragedy. For an age increasingly concerned with explaining the fabric of its own life, the world of myth provided a ready-made stage, complete with characters, on which to enact its notions of man's physical and spiritual struggles. Through Aeschylus, Sophocles and other dramatists, the Greeks were confronted in concise and vivid form with some of the propositions they had come to feel instinctively—the balance between constraint and freedom,

man's capacity to excel in adversity, their own innate awareness of destiny.

Thus through the theater, through art, through literature,
and through all stages of social and individual evolution, Greek
mentality was steeped in the dye of myth.

Tyrants, among Others 4

The high days of the Achaeans ended abruptly and dismally. About 1200 B.C., their domination of southern Greece was terminated by a wave of rough but determined invaders, the Dorians.

The migration of the Dorians, who fell on the Achaeans from the north, was yet another repercussion of the great tribal upheaval in Asia and Europe. They came originally from the valley of the Danube, following the rivers Morava and Vardar through the mountains to Thessaly and into the Balkan Peninsula. As they shouldered their way toward warmer lands, scattering, slaying or subduing the weaker folk in their path, the Dorians assimilated blood and habits from those they overran, pouring into southern Greece like the overflow from some immense melting pot.

For the next few centuries, events there are wrapped in obscurity. The light of the Heroic Age is extinguished, and the gloom filled with many struggling shadows—far too many to survive on the limited resources of the scattered plains. In the scramble for subsistence, civilized things were trampled underfoot. Many people fled overseas, to the Aegean Islands and the Asiatic coast, which, as time passed, abounded in offshoots of the peninsula communities. The old names of the regions between the Hellespont and the isle of Rhodes—Aeolis, Ionia and Doris—echo the waves of migrants which flooded into Greece from the north.

Slowly a pattern reemerged from the free-for-all. Separated by hill and sea, the more resourceful of the inhabitants began to consolidate in small groups, each fighting for its patch of productive land under a local war chief. The successors of these chiefs became the landed aristocrats.

Circumstance had obliged many people with no seafaring tradition to learn the maritime skills of the Achaeans, just as the Achaeans had learned them from the Cretans. When warlike people take to the sea the first thing they normally turn to is piracy. As they mellow, they discover that trading is safer and more lucrative. So it was with these new Greeks.

With trade came social and political changes. As the merchants prospered, they formed the core of a middle or commercial class which, being independent of the soil, was independent of the aristocratic landlords. This enviable station roused the more ambitious of the poorer classes to question the yoke of the nobility and seek a larger share in goods and government.

It is an odd law of life, supported by history, that the impoverished and the affluent are equally conservative. The well-to-do see no need for change; the poor fear it because, in their experience, the only alternative to a bare living is starvation. Radicalism, the desire to change things for the better, stems from those in transition, those who have risen from the paralysis of poverty but have not yet acquired the indifference of prosperity. They are blind neither to the injustice nor the potential, and they want to alter things. That is why, paradoxical though it seems, oppressed people tend to revolt not at the times of their most hopeless deprivation but in the early stages of reform, just as things begin to change for the better.

Thus the people in Greece, having tolerated the mastery of the aristocrats for generations, became restless when the glimpse of a different life was offered by the appearance of a middle class.

The lords and princes sniffed danger. One of the ways they sought to preserve their power was by packing off the discontented to new settlements overseas—a deliberate system of colonization which, in the first half of the eighth century, began to reshape the world of Greek expatriates originally created by random flight. And, of course, they used their soldiers. But the old style of rule had been perilously undermined. Kingdoms and aristocracies fell to popular movements.

The Greeks now discovered one of the awkward facts about people's revolutions—namely, that they cannot be achieved without leaders, and that once those leaders have power they very easily become the new autocrats.

To distinguish the rulers enthroned by the upheaval from the old hereditary kings, they were called tyrants, the new form of monarchy being a *tyrannis*, or tyranny. The word in itself was morally neutral. It did not imply that the ruler was bad or cruel—indeed, many of the Greek tyrants were enlightened men whose hard, practical regimes secured a peace in which social amenities developed. But the system was repugnant to those who had tasted freedom, and the tyrants became even less popular than the aristocrats.

As trade flourished and influential merchant families arose to add their weight to the discontent of the citizens in general, the new kings were gradually shorn of their wide powers.

It happened in stages, by no means in all cities at the same time. First, the armies by which the tyrants upheld their authority were torn from the royal command and placed under elected supremos, or polemarchs. Next, in many cases the tyrants were succeeded by archons, or regents, who, though resembling kings, were elected by the community from the great families. The principle of election, though initially very limited in practice, was profound in implication. Henceforward, those who governed became increasingly under obligation to the public.

In the beginning, election was for life, but it was only a matter of time before elections for the office of archon were held every ten years, and then annually. The electors were now the real power. As their number spread from a privileged few to the mass of free men, the citizens became the government, and government by the people *(demos)* was known as democracy. True, monarchs retained power beside republics in certain places, while tyrants and aristocrats remained a threat to democracy throughout the history of ancient Greece. But after the seventh century B.C., the citizens of the Greek world had more and more to say in their own affairs, and of none was this truer than the citizens of Athens.

In the year of Marathon, 490 B.C., Athenian democracy was threatened not only by the Persian might of Darius but by a more insidious enemy within its own walls. From the outset, the democratic system, with its relative tolerance of inconsistent views and factions, had a built-in security problem, for if people were free to advocate their own policies, what was to prevent the suppression of democracy becoming one of them? The answer was that tolerance had its limits and that the people, as well as despots, could make things unpleasant for those who opposed their rule.

Socrates, a voluble and unsparing critic of the democracy of his day, was eventually charged and sentenced to death, ostensibly for "corrupting the young" and "impiety," but really for challenging the system. In the manner of the time, he was obliged to drink a fatal dose of poison. Nevertheless, he was given a public trial by jury and a patient hearing, and was sentenced only reluctantly after he refused to apologize—options few princely rulers would have granted him. Despots gave short shrift to potential subversives. Democracies, while drawing a danger line, undoubtedly offered malcontents more latitude.

Consequently, when news of the Persian invasion reached Athens, the fears of its citizens were not eased by an awareness of those among them who saw advantage in an enemy victory and who might even assist it by treachery. A fuller understanding of such fears demands a brief sketch of the city's political history.

Athens, with the invitingly defensible pile of the Acropolis, and its protective ring of mountains, was a typical Mycenaean stronghold, and many remains of that culture have been found at the site and in surrounding Attica.

According to Greek legend, the wife of King Minos of

Crete, having succumbed to the virility of a bull, gave birth to the Minotaur, half-man, half-beast, a monster that lived on human flesh. Each year, the story had it, Athens was required to provide a portion of its youth to gratify the monster's appetite. At length, Theseus, a prince of the ruling house, resolved to end the grisly process. Volunteering to join the intended victims, Theseus slew the Minotaur, freed Athens from tribute to Crete and established the government of Attica in his home city. The legend, drawing on memories of the Cretan empire and Cretan bullfighting, probably recalls an authentic stage in the growth of early Athens.

Much later, when the Dorians were overwhelming the Achaeans, Athens rallied to a fugitive prince from Pylos (in the western Peloponnesus), whose successors withheld power from the invaders with some success. Indeed, Attica remained comparatively free of Dorian influence, perhaps, in part, because its land was less fertile than elsewhere in Greece.

At all events, the last of the Pylian kings, Codros, died securing the Acropolis from the Dorians, after which Athens dispensed with monarchs in favor of archons. With the archons came election. But since the archons could be elected only by and from the noble families, the result did little, at first, to better the common lot.

While large numbers of people, reduced to destitution by the great influx of immigrants, sold themselves into slavery to meet their debts, the noble landowners prospered under a government chiefly concerned with their own interests. So harsh were the laws against the poor—according to the historian Plutarch, the penalty for almost every crime was death —that the name of Draco, the seventh-century Athenian statesman who first committed them to writing, became synonymous with severity.

In fact, whatever we may mean by Draconian, Draco was a reforming influence. By tabulating the laws, he at least let the people know where they stood. He also extended political rights to all citizens able to serve as guardsmen—that is, rich enough to provide the arms and equipment of heavy infantry at their own expense. Still, the majority of free men were without representation in government, and the discontent was loud and dangerous.

By the beginning of the sixth century, tension between the nobles and the people was so critical that a special mediator with extraordinary powers of legislation was appointed. This official, Solon, was well chosen. He had an aristocratic pedigree, but had gone into business as a merchant because the family had spent its wealth giving help to distressed friends. Acceptable to all classes, Solon enjoyed a reputation for civic-mindedness and worldly wisdom. In his own words, he set himself to give "the mass of the people such status as fitted their need" while protecting the "splendor and state" of the nobility. First, he produced a milder code of laws to supersede Draco's, and provided even the poorest Athenian citizen with a vote in the government. Then he created an administrative council of four hundred members, a hundred from each of the four ancient tribes of Attica which were led by the great families.

Solon's formula was a big stride toward democracy, but nobody could satisfy both the pretensions of the aristocrats and the aspirations of the people at a single stroke. The former resented popular suffrage; the latter resented the prominence of the old tribes, and hence the nobility, in government.

Conflict continued, but in a new pattern. Now there were three distinct political parties. These parties, broadly identified as the plainsmen, the shoremen and the hillsmen, were at once regional and economic in origin. By and large, the party of the productive plains was that of the landowners, aristocratic, conservative; the party of the barren hills was that of the underprivileged freemen, extreme democrats; the party of the shore embraced the trading middle classes, who might be termed moderates. In detail the situation was more complex. Just as there were poor men on the plains with reason to support the aristocrats, so there were powerful families in the hills ready to lead the democrats. Among these hill nobles was a certain Pisistratus, who took upon himself the championship of the underprivileged. After many years of sparring, the three-cornered contest was interrupted by a dramatic blow. Having secured predominance within the hill party, Pisistratus overthrew the elected government and made himself tyrant of Athens.

Pisistratus ruled, with a few intervals, from 560 to 527, a tyrant representing democrats—one of those bizarre contortions which defy definition in the normal terms of politics. Anomalous he might be, but his government, lenient, just and popular, clearly worked. It was not until he died, and his sons succeeded him, that the machine Pisistratus had established began to run amok.

If it is the nature of absolute government to react narrowly and oppressively in the long run, Hippias and Hipparchus proved orthodox. When Hipparchus was killed in the name of liberation, Hippias shocked Athens with a reign of suppression, extortion and executions. Tyranny took on a new and black meaning for Athenians. Finally, in 510, with Spartan support, the opponents of Hippias banished him and his family from Attica.

The Pisistratids had fallen, and with them the hill party. Popular support had swung to the shore party, the new hope of the frustrated democrats. Its leader, Cleisthenes, may be regarded as the decisive architect of Athenian democracy. By the constitution of Solon, the people had acquired a limited share of political power. Through the legislation of Cleisthenes, the constitution was transformed to give them supreme power.

Cleisthenes realized that the old political ties of clan and region were obstacles to progress. He decided, therefore, on a system to diminish local and family influence. Roughly, it worked like this: (1) he divided Attica into three areas, more or less corresponding to the regions which had given rise to the parties of plain, hill and shore; (2) he divided each of these areas into ten sections, or *trittyes;* (3) he then replaced the ancient tribes with ten new and quite artificial tribes, a tribe comprising three sections, or *trittyes.*

The scheme was astute in that each of the new tribes drew one of its three *trittyes* from each of the original areas, plain, hill and shore. In this way, no tribe contained two groups from the same district. The regional cliques, with their impulse to create discord, were most effectively weakened. At the same time, Cleisthenes reconstituted the administrative body: the council or senate. Under Solon this had contained four hundred members from the old tribes. Cleisthenes increased the council to five hundred, fifty from each of the new tribes, considerably widening its membership.

These reforms of Cleisthenes were popular, but since all reform arouses opposition, and the opposition to popular reform is invariably well entrenched, Cleisthenes introduced a device to protect his democracy against subversion. Somewhat primitive in technique, it was known as ostracism. At certain intervals, any citizen had the right to present an *ostrakon,* a piece of earthenware bearing the name of some influential person he considered a threat to the security of the state. If a sufficient number of complaints were put forward, an unpopular figure might be ordered to leave the country for ten years.

Ostracism, regarded more as a preventive measure than a punishment, encouraged those who opposed the system to air their views prudently. It could not, of course, eliminate such views, and there was always a body of citizens which saw its interests best served by some other form of government. For example, there were men who had enjoyed the patronage of tyranny and favored the reinstatement of the exiled Hippias.

In 490 the presence of these antidemocrats in the community became a very real source of treachery.

For now, as the enemy lay at Marathon, Hippias, the former tyrant, having pledged himself to Darius, stepped ashore with the Persian commanders.

5 The City

Mobilization notices were posted beside the statues of the heroes in the agora, the public place between the civic buildings. Groups of men hastened through the city with burnished bronze helmets and round shields decorated with allegoric devices. Every Athenian male between the ages of twenty and sixty was liable for military service. With the Persians on the coast, each made for his station. The war councils conferred. The warriors mustered. The dust of Athens was stirred by marching feet.

Bystanders, young and old, watched the preparations. At wells and market stalls, in nurseries and kitchens, while spinning, dancing or tending sepulchers, women paused to ponder the rattle of armor, the rasp of commanders. Crop-haired servant girls, the smart wives of the bourgeoisie and apprehensive mothers—none can have ignored the implications of a Persian victory. For it was in their beds that the "barbarians" would seize the first prize of conquest, and on their children that the brand of the East would burn indelibly.

While husbands, sons and fathers strode off with slung swords, the women of Athens made supplication, seeking strength in their gods and heroic precedent. The future of their world was in the balance. On the fortunes of that bronze-clad band of citizens—and a solitary envoy to Sparta—depended all that seemed to them right and desirable: the unique and fondly cherished Athenian way of life. By this the people of Athens did not understand anything resembling the materialistic values of modern society.

Most citizens worked hard for a fairly meager income which allowed no scope for extravagance. Even the prosperous were singularly uncovetous of worldly goods. Their homes reflected little of the opulence common to the rich of other ages. They kept servants to save themselves from mundane tasks, but filled their leisure with interests which, on the whole, did not cost much.

They were ardent sport followers, especially of track and field events. They gave time to unremunerative civic duties. They enjoyed themselves at the symposium, a popular form of after-dinner party where men drank, listened to music, watched dancing and dallied with girls of versatile talents and accommodating virtue.

Above all, they simply talked—talked politics, talked philosophy, talked theater, talked religion and, of course, talked sport. If they rolled home to the arms of their wives a little drunk from the symposium, it was as much on their own heady eloquence as on the Attic wine.

The Athenian housewife who had bread, barley meal, olive oil, figs and honey in her larder, with perhaps a little fish or some cheese made from goat's milk, considered herself well-off —as, indeed, she was, compared with most of humanity at the time.

Whatever else Athens was preparing to defend against the Persians, it was not the right to rich food and costly trappings. The soil of Attica was thin and shallow, and the average citizen existed on a frugal if wholesome diet, mostly vegetarian. His clothing was light and basic; his home, if aesthetically agreeable, austere. Such meeting places as the theater and the political assembly were roofless, with seating of bare stone. Fundamentally, the Athenian was grateful for a temperate climate conducive to outdoor life, a translucent atmosphere which promoted the shapes and colors of nature, and an abundance of rock and clay with which to celebrate these in the plastic arts.

Geographically there was plenty to stir his spirit in his surroundings. From the elevation of the Pnyx, the stony seat of his "parliament," the citizen could gaze south upon the silver sheen of the Saronic Gulf, east upon purple-hued mountains aromatic with wild thyme, north to the sunny, bee-haunted gardens of the Academy. Taking in the city itself, with its gymnasia, fountains, temples, its cleanly proportioned public halls and private dwellings, its tree-shaded spaces and ubiquitous statuary, it was not surprising that the Athenian assembly was moved quickly to patriotic fervor.

Four or five miles to the southwest lay the city's port, Piraeus, and beside it the Bay of Phalerum. Here emptied the river Cephisus which, traced inland, broke into three courses before reaching Athens. One, the Cephisus proper, passed the conurbation to the west, through groves of olive trees. Another, the Ilissus, passed south before sweeping through the eastern suburbs. The third and central course, the Eridanus, went right through the city.

The city was a rocky, dusty place, "badly laid out," declared the writer Dicaearchus, "on account of its antiquity," but it had a craggy grandeur set off by the geometric purity of its buildings. At the heart of Athens, the towering Acropolis, nearly 200 feet high and 1,000 by 500 feet in length and breadth, had become less a fortress now than a sacred place, covered with altars, statues and sanctuaries. On its western terraces, a secondary height known as Areopagus, the "Hill of Mars," had once been the meeting point for the old council of nobles. Four centuries later, St. Paul would stand here, or hereabouts, survey the countless tributes Athens had raised to its gods and heroes, and deplore the "superstitious" nature of its citizens. "God dwelleth not in temples made with hands," he would tell them, an observation which did not, as we now know, stop innumerable early Christians from flocking into churches in search of beneficent miracles. To the north of Areopagus, between the foot of the hill and the Eridanus, stretched the agora, the site of markets, parades and many other gatherings. Surrounded by stately colonnades, it was planted with plane trees for grace and refreshing shade.

Athens inspires, but it was not Utopia. It is easy to exagger-
ate its size and amenities. In fact, the city was rather less than
a square mile in area. Its houses, numbered by the historian
Xenophon at ten thousand, were generally flat-roofed, stuc-
coed or plastered and, according to a later writer, rather
"mean."

"Street" is perhaps a flattering term for the thoroughfares,
most of which were mere paths or passages and few were paved.
Since these were commonly the repository of slops and garbage
from the neighboring dwellings, the metropolitan roadmen
must have had a thankless task. Aristophanes complained of
the hazards of night walking, an exercise endangered by pools
of mud and fetid house-waste. Public drainage, though partially
covered, was inadequate, and disease menacing. The writing of
Thucydides reveals at least one plague in Athens of widespread
and lingering horror.

If the Athenians cared more for their public buildings and
statues, for philosophic and social intercourse than for sanita-
tion, they would not be unique among creative peoples of any
age. Yet, in fact, they possessed social services of a remarkably
advanced kind. At a time when most of Europe lived in primitive huts and wore the pelts of beasts, Athens had a water
system, based on natural springs, incorporating such engineering feats as the reservoir, conduit and aqueduct. The springs
themselves—the most famous was the Callirrhoe, the Fair-
Flowing, close to the southern gates—were embellished with
fountains and wellheads which enhanced both their utility and
ornamental value. Here the women gathered to fill their urns
and share their fears as the men marched out to meet the
enemy. More normally, their gossip sparkled and gushed like
the fountains.

Despite the protests of our nineteenth-century forebears,
those earnest advocates of the Greek virtues, Athenian women
were worldly, witty and assertive. It so happened that our
pedantic ancestors of Victorian vintage, though much impressed by the heroic aspirations they culled from classic litera-

ture, were shocked by sexual freedom and frankness. Keeping their own womenfolk in a form of permanently adolescent seclusion from the world of adult relationships, they averred stoutly that the ancient Greeks did the same. Abetted by the fact that Plato, that most quoted of Greeks, was exceptionally ignorant of the fair sex, the notion has persisted of the sheltered, docile Athenian woman, unspotted by the rude world. A battery of Greek writers who, unlike Plato, really understood women makes it nonsense.

In the works of Aeschylus, Sophocles, Euripides and, above all, Aristophanes, Athenian wives and daughters are shown abounding in ideas and initiative, running households and husbands, letting their hair down at festivals, frequenting the theater, inspiring sons, coping with lovers, gaily discoursing, sometimes friskily bibulous. Aristophanes's brilliant comedy, *Lysistrata,* in which the women of Greece reveal their ultimate strength by refusing to go to bed with their men, is a timeless comment on the power and wit of the human female.

The simple fact that women attended the Athenian theater suggests a remarkable ease and freedom between the sexes, for many Greek plays would have made a cavalry sergeant blush at their bawdiness, and would be considered quite unsuitable for mixed audiences even now in large areas of society.

The men of Athens may have liked to get away from their wives on occasions, but Attic femininity was far from neglected. On the contrary, it was exalted. Athenian art is preoccupied with the celebration of womanhood: women at the wellhouse, at the shoemaker's, at the loom; women nursing and playing with children; women, nakedly beautiful, dressing, washing, bathing at the swimming pool. Vase paintings capture them devotedly at all stages of their lives: cute little bridesmaids chattering importantly, flirtatious girls eyeing handsome boyfriends, vain brides smugly consulting the looking-glass, bereaved wives at the tombs of warrior husbands, comely matrons, sagacious dowagers, knowing crones. It is necessary merely to glance at the Acropolis to confirm the vein of femi-

nism in Athenian culture. Embodied in the shrines and sanctuaries of Athena, Artemis, Gaea and others, the goddesses
seem to have outweighed the gods there, just as the marble
statues of girls on the hill outnumbered those of boys and men.

Pictures of women and men together—talking, sporting,
relaxing—are pleasingly free of self-consciousness. For instance, a vase painting made some ten years before Marathon,
and still surviving, shows two young men reclining on cushions
with their girl companions. All four figures are naked, the men
crowned with flowers, the long hair of the girls swathed with
ribbon. One girl kneels beside her boy, stretching her arms to
him. The other couple make love, the man supporting the girl's
head with his left arm, caressing her buttocks with his right
hand as she smiles at him. The unaffected frankness of the
portrait is underlined by the fact that the names of those
portrayed are elegantly inscribed beside them.

Fifth-century Athens, though more sophisticated and formal
in its sex relationships than Heroic Greece, was no more prud-
ish. Like most of Hellas, it had its brothels and its streetwalkers.
But such crudities were mainly for visiting foreigners. For the
citizen, Athens had evolved something different, and very
Athenian, the *hetaira*.

Hetairai (literally, companions, though the word implied
some professionalism) were cultivated, often highly educated
girls, usually from beyond Attica, who sought their careers in
the male world, perhaps as models, business women or simply
as accomplished opportunists. Invited to the type of social
gatherings to which men did not bring their wives, the *hetairai's* role was variously intellectual, decorative and passionate.
They initiated young men in the arts of love, graced drinking
parties with their conversation and beauty, and solaced older
men with their practiced charms. A few—among them As-
pasia, mistress of the statesman Pericles—became great courte-
sans or, like Phryne, a creature of celebrated proportions,
gained renown by posing for famous artists and sculptors.

For all the fascination of such ladies, however, there is no doubt the deepest respect and affection of the Athenian male was for his wife, the mistress of his home and mother of his children—a fact strongly attested during the century of Marathon by the large number of marble tributes erected to women in the city by their husbands.

If *she* was a bit of a tippler, and took an occasional lover; if *he* was inclined to be a bore about politics, and had an eye for pretty flute-girls, there seems to have been a tolerant acceptance of such individual inclinations in Athenian society. After all, one could hardly lead a secret life in so small a dominion, especially one whose people lived so publicly and sociably.

So far, this view of Athens on the eve of Marathon has avoided an odd contradiction: the fact that the democratic Athenians kept slaves. Not all of them, and probably not the majority. But a substantial proportion of the citizens possessed a slave or two apiece, while a few had a very large number. (One rich man, Nicias, kept a thousand, hiring the bulk of them out as laborers.)

Embarrassingly enough for those who would idealize Athens, more than half the people in the city were not Athenians at all in the strict sense, but men and women of servile status and largely foreign extraction, bought and owned by their masters, and lacking any voice in the government.

It is tempting to dismiss the anomaly lightly, observing that no ancient society was without slaves. Yet the point begs the question. No other ancient society was governed by the people. Greek society laid unique emphasis on liberty and freedom of expression, on a straight and sincere approach to social justice. The Athenian in particular was ready to apply his reason to public matters without fear or prejudice. Why not to slavery? Was there some kind of conspiracy to ignore the subject?

Hardly. None could accuse such penetrating commentators as Socrates, Plato or Aristotle of compromise or humbug. Few have been less addicted to hypocrisy or readier to declare their opinions unequivocally. Yet nobody spoke out against slavery. Quite clearly, the Greeks saw nothing wrong in it.

Areas of social blindness in otherwise enlightened communities are not uncommon. Indeed, it is doubtful if any popular system, however radical, has failed to preserve certain attitudes, often entirely inconsistent with its rational ethos, on the strength of unwritten tradition and inherited emotion. Such areas are generally held to be outside the forum of public debate. The evolution of Greek affairs appears to have cast slavery in this category.

Slavery was as much a part of the conservatism underlying Athenian democracy as was, for example, a form of justice which, for all its liberal mechanism, could still force those who flouted the unwritten code to drink hemlock.

Nowadays, all slavery is seen to be odious, but it cannot be denied that for the slaves of some peoples life was a good deal better than for the slaves of others. In this context, the slaves of Athens were fortunate. So lenient, it seems, was their treatment, so unstressed their subservience, that the Spartans, who practiced a rigorous mastership, regarded the comparative permissiveness of Athens as dangerous. An Athenian document connected with the works of Xenophon sets out to apprise the Spartans of the advantages of giving slaves incentives, including payment, and to show that this enhances rather than detracts from state security.

A stroll through the streets of Athens would have revealed little distinction between slaves and freemen. The slave wore no differentiating style of dress (though female slaves did wear their hair short). He was normally of white stock, often a prisoner of war by origin, perhaps acquired by traders in Asia Minor or the northern Balkans, or a descendant of slave parents born in a Greek household.

The domestic slave lived much as a member of the family, sharing its food and religious observances, receiving its nursing care when sick, and even welcomed with confetti as a new arrival.

True, punishments for laziness, running away, and other misdemeanors might be harsh. He could be whipped, pilloried and placed in fetters. In most cases, however, only his master was entitled to chastise him, and a citizen was answerable to the law for cruelty. Public opinion was a strong deterrent to ill-treatment. It wasn't done in respectable circles to be nasty to one's servants. Only an ill-bred man, observed Plato, would abuse his slave.

Whatever went on elsewhere, no Athenian slave, Xenophon assures us, would dream of cringing or dodging away from a citizen in the street. Of course, the view is patronizing and complacent. Hundreds of slaves, hired out to shipyards, mines and sword and shield foundries, were rough, backward fellows with very little hope of advancement. Though paid by the industries, their wages went largely to their owners, the slave retaining about a sixth of what he earned. His chances of saving enough from this type of employment to buy his freedom—a theoretical prospect—were not bright.

On the other hand, the slave employed as a craftsman—carpenters, cobblers, potters, sculptors, goldsmiths and others were frequently enslaved men—enjoyed a better outlook. His pay appears to have equaled that for a freeman in the same job. Indeed, distinctions between slaves and citizens on an occupational basis were seldom emphatic. Probably the great majority of Athenian citizens worked hard for a living, often side by side with slaves, and certainly many performed jobs more menial than did a number of skilled slaves. It was not unknown for poor freemen to seek domestic employment, the lot of the common slave. Conversely, some of the best architects and engineers in the city were slaves. Their chances of buying, or being awarded freedom, were considerable. One slave, Pasion, became a banker and left a fortune which included an armaments factory.

In one vocation slaves held a virtual monopoly. Apart from its officers, the Athenian police force was entirely slave-manned, traditionally by Scythians from the north of the Black Sea. Armed with bows, its members kept order at public gatherings and implemented magisterial instructions.

All in all, it may be seen that preconceived ideas of slavery engendered by later history are not helpful in comprehending the situation in Athens. Apart from a closer affinity of race and color between slave and master in ancient Greece, the democratic sentiment and relative absence of greed and pomposity in the Athenian citizen set him nearer his slaves than the aristocratic planters of the Deep South, the avaricious merchant-adventurers of Britain, Holland and Portugal, the heartless Arab and Turkish traders, the cruel bigots of the Spanish empire, or the arrogant masters of imperial Rome.

That is not to condone slavery in any guise. The Greek assumption that some men were born to be masters, others to obey, was a pernicious one, and none the better for having been perpetuated by many down to modern times. What set the Athenian apart as a slave owner was that he pursued the assumption, characteristically, with a certain grace.

Like slavedom, citizenship in Athens was mainly conferred by birth. Having struggled long and painfully for their equality of rights, the Athenians jealously preserved the fruits of the struggle for their children. Those born of citizen parents were citizens; those otherwise born remained, with some exceptions, beyond the pale.

A resident foreigner—and there were many in Athens, mostly merchants or their agents—might spend his life in the city, liable to taxation, military service and Athenian law, and still have no vote or voice in politics, no hope of public office. Rich he might be, or respected, but that made no difference. He was an alien, an "outlander," and not a citizen.

Occasionally, the sovereign people would be generous. An alien who had proved an outstanding benefactor to the state, or a slave who had rendered conspicuous public service, might be granted citizenship. But the privilege was never bestowed capriciously. Two public assemblies had to approve the measure, after which an inquiry could be ordered into the character of the candidate and the claims made for him before the sanction was ratified.

Short of such uncommon circumstances, citizenship depended not only on having a citizen father and mother, but on their having been betrothed and married with full formalities. When a citizen birth was registered, its legitimacy had to be sworn by the father and investigated. A further examination might be required in the eighteenth year of a youth's life, the time of his nomination to the roll of adult citizens. Even then, he had to do a period of military conscription before, at twenty, he could attend the assembly and vote as an equal of his father, and a further ten years before he was eligible for the council.

Such was the law. As in all states, there were infringements, some of them scandalous. The satirists were not loath to make play of it. An occasional greasing of palms, they alluded, and some rich outsider might happily discover his name on the electoral rolls. Aristophanes was quite prepared to provide names. Again, political pressures might open a back door. Later, perhaps, public outrage would prevail and there would be purges.

Yet, on the whole, the Athenian respected the laws, for they were of his own making. The state was a cooperative venture for the common good, and those inclined to abuse it faced the loss of their privileges. Citizenship was not immutable. A citizen could be degraded and disfranchised for a number of antisocial activities, including accepting bribes in the course of public duty. So penalized, he was no longer entitled to speak in the assembly, hold any office, bring an action at law, or even appear in the public square. Reinstatement was exceedingly difficult to obtain.

What, then, were the attractions of this much-prized citizenship? Certainly not enrichment or aggrandizement. On the contrary, having acknowledged the injustices of despotism, oligarchy and class rule, the Athenians were concerned about preventing undue power or wealth falling to one man or one group.

The great privileges of citizenship, as democrats saw it, were equal rights and opportunities, of which equal obligations and responsibilities were held to be self-evident corollaries. Not only was every citizen equal before the law, but a real attempt was made to give everyone (that is, every male citizen; women did not have a formal role in public matters) an equal share in legislating, administering and dispensing justice.

In most modern states, such an aim would be ludicrous. Athens was small enough to make it feasible. Scale was the essential difference between Greek democracy and its successors. The Athenian deliberative assembly, for instance, was not composed of representatives of the electors, as in later democracies, but of the entire electorate—as, indeed, was the judiciary.

It is an eloquent comment on the public spirit of Athens that its citizens, in the thousands, regularly sacrificed earnings and leisure to sit on stone seats, often in exhausting heat, sometimes wind and rain, listening to parliamentary debate and lawsuit. It seemed to them no more than sensible. Either they governed themselves or someone else would govern them. For those who failed to attend the assembly without good cause, they had a term, *idiotes*, which persists in Western usage as "idiot."

The Greek approached public affairs as his own affairs. While believing in the power of the gods to shape his destiny, he saw no salvation in abandoning politics to providence. Social problems were caused by men, and by men they must be resolved.

In administration the ideal of shared government was a tricky one. There could hardly be enough executive offices for everyone, nor could everyone be fit to hold a post. The citizens did their best. Having created a very wide range of offices, they made the term of office annual, with a provision that nobody should hold the same civil post more than once. To ensure the impartial selection of candidates, they were picked by drawing beans from a pot: black beans were void; a white bean was a winner. Unfortunately, a white bean was no guarantee of a suitable applicant. So there were safeguards.

For a start, the totally unfit were unlikely to apply for appointment. If they did not know their own limitations, others would inform them. In a small community, personal capacities were widely known, and public opinion is a potent force. Beyond which, an officer's fitness could be challenged on the announcement of his selection, or his performance impeached in the course of his incumbency. In the case of certain offices where special ability was critical—military commanders, engineering appointments, high financial posts—selection was restricted to those with the proper skills.

There was also a check on individual performance in the fact that Athenian administration was very much a board, or committee, operation. There was a harbor board, a road board, a public-buildings board, a board of chief magistrates and of treasury officers, police commissioners and temple stewards; a board for weights and measures, food supplies, the public games and so on. Mutual supervision was considerable.

Obviously, the sytem had drawbacks. Among others, diffusion of responsibility does not make for quick decisions. But it did two things most efficiently: it heightened the electorate's sense of involvement in government and the community; and it produced an aggregate of administrative experience in the assembly which was extremely valuable when the time came to legislate. A large number of people knew the problems of governing at first hand. Power, then, lay with the citizens. Forty times a year, they assembled for ordinary parliamentary meetings, apart from which they could be summoned by crier or trumpet to extraordinary sessions.

There was, however, a limit to the time the electorate as a body could spend on public business without disrupting private affairs and the economy. Each year, therefore, a council or senate of five hundred citizens, all over the age of thirty, was picked by lot to handle state matters in daily detail, and to sift and prepare items for the assembly. Though the council's decision alone had no validity, no legislative proposal could come before the assembly undiscussed by the council. Its five hundred members were divided into ten sections of fifty which, in turn, stood at immediate availability as a duty executive. During its duty tour, this executive was responsible for all initial approaches to the council, for convening council meetings and for summoning the assembly. To maintain close contact, its members dined in a special hall at public expense. Every day, one of their number was picked by lot to be president—a fleeting moment of prominence which doubtless warmed the heart of the civic-minded Athenian, but would scarcely have delighted any self-respecting tyrant. When his twenty-four-hour reign was over, the Athenian citizen would not again be eligible for the post.

That was the nearest thing Athens had to a head of state.

On the second day of his exertions, the runner Philippides passed Mount Parthenium, and entering the land of Laconia, in the east of the Peloponnesus, perceived Sparta sprawled beneath the snow-capped range of Taygetus. Descending from the rocky passes to the sword-shaped valley before him, he covered the last lap of his tortuous journey within forty-eight hours of departing Athens. A hundred and fifty mountainous miles in two days—it was a feat in the best tradition of Greek athleticism.

Through the valley, from its source in northern hills to its southern egress in the Gulf of Laconia, rippled the Eurotas, a shallow, sandy stream banked with oleander and tall reeds. Gratefully the runner must have steeped his bruised feet in its waters.

Sparta, otherwise known as Lacedaemon, the capital of this land, was an open city—more precisely, a conglomerate of villages—on one of the most fertile plains in all Greece. Around it, in place of fortifications, grew figs, olives, mulberries, melons and other fruit.

The Spartans liked to boast that they needed no bastions, that the valor of their sons was ample protection. It was not an idle claim. Looking back to the clouded morrow of the Dorian invasion, one fact stands out with unusual clarity: namely, that of all the people of southern Greece the men of Sparta were unexcelled as warriors.

By the end of the seventh century, they had conquered the neighboring, and richer, kingdom of Messenia, reducing most of its Dorian and Achaean population to serfdom. In the sixth century Sparta placed its dominance in the Peloponnesus beyond dispute. Of the other lands south of the Corinthian isthmus, Argos lost part of its border to Sparta; Arcadia saw one of its chief cities, Tegea, made politically dependent on Sparta; Elis required the protection of Sparta for its presidency of the Olympic Games.

Not only did the Spartans head an effective if loose confederacy of all the Dorian states except Argos, but they were widely recognized outside the Peloponnesus as the foremost people in Hellas. Which was none the less remarkable, since, like the Athenians, there were very few of them—probably not more than ten thousand fighting men at any time. Moreover, with this force they had to control an overwhelmingly numerous and often unruly subject population, as well as to pursue campaigns outside their own territories. To achieve this, the whole Spartan system aimed at military efficiency. Elsewhere, the army was part of the Greek state; in Sparta the army *was* the state —a community of full-time warriors who, as one ancient remarked pithily, were "the only men in the world for whom war brought a respite from training for it."

The Spartan life would have been impossible without others to do the work. Again like the Athenians, the Spartans were a governing minority in their country. Beneath them were a free but voteless middle class called *Perioikoi*, or town-dwellers, and the Helots, or serfs, the descendants of earlier inhabitants conquered by the Dorians.

Philippides was not concerned with the *Perioikoi* or the Helots. They might augment the regular army in battle, but they had no powers of decision. His mission lay with the ruling warrior caste, the true Spartans. What he thought of them is a mystery. It may be that he was picked not just as a runner but as someone who got on well with the elite of Laconia. If so, he was not typical of his fellow citizens. Many democratic Athenians thought the Spartans a pretty dreadful lot. Most Athenians considered the Spartan system stiff and ultraconservative. The embodiment in its government of a couple of kings, one from each of two equally dignified royal houses, and a council of aged noblemen smacked of aristocratic power and the bad old times.

In fact, real power at Sparta was vested in a board of five magistrates, freely elected each year by an assembly in which every Spartan warrior who had reached the age of thirty had a right to vote. While the kings retained their tradition of leadership in battle, it was the magistrates, called ephors, who controlled foreign policy and effectively kept a check on home affairs.

Today, "the Spartan life" evokes a picture of austerity, discipline and harsh endurance. Like many generalizations about groups of people—"Americans are rich," "Latins are passionate"—it is a selective view.

Sparta was conformist, and proud of it. From birth the Spartan's way of life was determined by the state, even to the extent of his survival in the first place. At a few days of age, every child was taken before a committee of old men which judged its bodily fitness to become a useful Spartan. If the infant was considered a poor physical specimen, it was carried to the mountains and left to die of exposure—a repugnant act which must, nevertheless, have saved much later suffering in an age ill-equipped to support the weakly and malformed. At the age of seven, the Spartan boy left his parents and embarked on a period of state supervision and schooling which continued until he was twenty. The instruction was distinctly strenuous and martial.

Plutarch, a later writer with a special interest in Spartan institutions, said that youths "learned only enough reading and writing to serve their turn; for the rest, their training was calculated to make them obey commands, endure hardships, and conquer in battle." These soldierly attributes, it seems, were stimulated by a plain diet, bare dormitories, waiting on seniors, hazing and an emphasis on games embracing the principles of warfare. Later, having graduated, the young man broadened his experience. Now there were hunting excursions into the wild hills, and police missions among the serfs of outlying territories. He also did his share of teaching and supervising his juniors.

Only at thirty was he admitted to the full rights of Spartan citizenship as a *peer*, and allocated an estate, or lot, on which his household would be supported by the labors of the local serfs. Still, though a gentlemanly existence, his was not a lazy life. "No man was allowed to live as he pleased," wrote Plutarch, "but, as in a military camp, had a set and constant regimen of public service, belonging entirely to country and not to self." There was no getting out of these state obligations. The Spartan peer mustered regularly for drill with his comrades, and dined each day at one of numerous mess halls, where the men established a fraternal relationship. An individual who did not meet with approval could be blackballed and forced to seek another mess. One may fairly imagine the members of these male clubs as possessing the general virtues and limitations of their profession: given to action rather than reflection, relatively unacquisitive, endowed with social integrity, sound if unimaginative. There is no evidence of unusual violence or aggressiveness. Indeed, Plutarch portrayed the Spartans as restrained, even in action:

> And when at last they were drawn up in battle array and the enemy was at hand, the king sacrificed the customary she-goat, commanded all the warriors to set garlands upon their heads and ordered the pipers to play the hymn . . .
>
> It was a grand and awesome sight when they marched in step with the rhythm of the flute, no gap in their ranks, no confusion in their souls, calmly and gladly moving to battle to the strains of their hymn. Neither fear nor excessive fury is likely to possess such men, but rather firm purpose, full of hope and courage, believing as they do that heaven is on their side . . .

And again:

> When they had conquered and routed the enemy, they pursued him far enough to secure the victory, then retired at once, thinking it ignoble and unworthy of Greece to butcher men who had given up the fight and left the field.

The Spartan, then, was no berserker or wild man but a highly trained member of a highly organized and primarily military society. Not until he was sixty, when his life as a warrior ended, was he free of training and campaigning. This much supports the portrait, so dear to regimentally inclined gentlemen through many generations and nations, of the stoic, dedicated prototype of the soldier-patriot. It also fits tidily with the view of Sparta and Athens as contrasting poles in Greek civilization: the authoritarian and the democratic, the conservative and the liberal, the manual and the cerebral, the prosaic and the elegant.

In truth, there was contrast in the cultures and organization of the two states. But it was not as tidy as all that. There were plenty of conservatives in Athens who must have seen much to envy in Spartan orderliness—and doubtless liberals in Sparta who dreamed of a less ordered life in Attica. There were poets in Sparta, just as there were military men in Athens, and no lack of gaiety and sport in the towns of Laconia. Pindar, the great lyric poet of ancient Greece, wrote of Sparta:

> There are councils of Elders,
> And young men's conquering spears,
> And dances, the Muse, and joyousness.

Nor was Sparta, as it sometimes seems, exclusively a man's world. Spartan women were conspicuously lively and venturesome. The state's responsibility for rearing children made for matronly freedom. The mortality rate of warrior husbands gave women, who could inherit estate in Sparta, economic power. In fact, they owned something like two-thirds of the private land.

Left on their own for long periods while the men were campaigning, Spartan women acquired independence and enterprise. Of course, they had no vote, but female suffrage is a very recent phenomenon, and not one, it can be added, with much apparent effect on women's freedom. Where women have obtained the vote in modern times, they have used it overwhelmingly to support men in government, and frequently men of reactionary character.

In real terms, few women in history have enjoyed as much liberty as those of ancient Sparta. In girlhood, they engaged in the same exercises as their brothers—running, wrestling, throwing the javelin, generally behaving like tomboys. There was no mollycoddling. In processions and dances, it was considered natural that the young of both sexes should go naked, taking pride in their fine physiques. Even when clothed, Spartan women wore their single garment, the Doric peplos, with negligent abandon, open from hem to waist for ease of movement—laying "bare her gleaming thigh," as Sophocles put it.

Other Greeks affected disapproval. The poet Ibycus, who hailed from a colony in Italy, called Spartan girls nymphomaniacs, and Euripides described their immodesty as intolerable. Plutarch commented more favorably on the erotic effect their dancing had on the young men.

Despite, or perhaps because of, her social ease, the sporting Spartan lass matured and married late, seldom far short of her twentieth birthday. Having installed her on the estate, her husband was soon off back to his messing club.

A habit of treating the bride as a mistress, to be loved by secret tryst, rather than as a wife in a more general sense appealed to the romance in the Spartan, and mock abduction was part of the marriage ceremonial.

But if the Spartans were romantic, they were not possessive, at least not in the exclusive sense. It appears to have been a mark of comradeship for a husband to allow another man of equal standing access to the wife's bed (so long as she approved of him), and to accept the possible offspring of the union. Sexual freedom was not slanted to favor men. Indeed, many women possessing the wherewithal to run two households took the opportunity of establishing a man in each. Since no social obloquy attached to such liberty, the concepts of illegitimacy, adultery and divorce as we know them were irrelevant.

During the Spartan conquest of Messenia, which dragged on for nearly twenty years, the women of the absent warriors consoled themselves by inviting the socially inferior *Perioikoi* into their bedrooms. When the Spartans returned from the war their homes were full of small, bright-eyed strangers—the *Partheniai*, or virgin-born, as these came to be classified. The warriors did not reproach their wives. Only one aspect of the affair troubled Sparta, and that was the ambiguous status of the *Partheniai*, who were neither full Spartans nor truly *bourgeoisie*. Eventually, the matter was quite simply resolved by sending them abroad to found a colony—Taras, in southern Italy, the modern Taranto.

Within the rigidity of the Spartan state there was a degree of tolerance and flexibility which many overtly liberal regimes of later times could not equal. Not only did it produce a military system rivaled in thoroughness by none save the Romans, but also some of the healthiest children and best-adjusted women in history.

If Athens gave her intellect to posterity, Sparta bequeathed some distinctive institutions. The British public school and Communist experiments in state responsibility for rearing children are among many social phenomena—both elitist and proletarian—that have borrowed inspiration from ancient Sparta.

The fact remains, however, that for all its special characteristics, Spartan culture was essentially the culture of Hellas. To Philippides, approaching across the vale of the Eurotas, the city

ahead held much more that was familiar than foreign to him
—much more in common with Athens than with the Persia of
Darius, the emperor of the "barbarians." It was on this reckoning that Athens sought Spartan aid. No state in Greece was
better able to provide it.

1. Part of the Ruins at Babylon. Photograph: Embassy of the Republic of Afghanistan, Iraqi Interests Section.

2. Ruins at Persepolis, once capital of Darius' empire. Photograph: Robin Hodson, Camera Press.

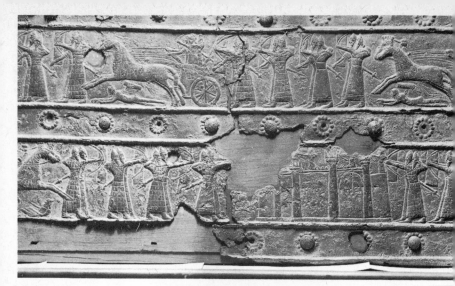

3. Assyrian Archers on the bronze band from the gate of Shalmaneser III. Photograph: British Museum.

4. The Stele of King Naram-Sin, showing the King of Akad leading warriors against Elam. Photograph: Musees Nationaux, Paris.

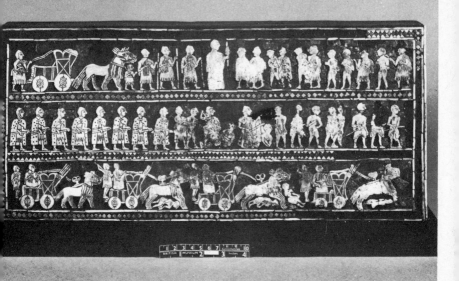

5. The Standard of Ur, showing Sumerian battle scenes using four-wheeled chariots. Photograph: British Museum.

6. Pillars of the Apadana Palace at Persepolis. Photograph: A. C. Barrington Brown, Camera Press.

7. Assurbanipal hunting on horseback—relief from the North Palace at Nineveh. Photograph: British Museum.

8. Cylinder seal impression of Darius hunting lion from a chariot, with winged symbol of Ahuramazda above. Photograph: British Museum.

9. Ruins at Delphi. Photograph: Bernard G. Silberstein, Camera Press.

10. Dancer and pipe player, a bowl painting. Photograph: British Museum.

11. Amphora painting of
Greek hoplite in war rega[lia]
Photograph: British Museum

12. 5th Century B.C. cup [by]
Brygos, depicting warri[ors]
battling at the sack of Tr[oy]
Photograph: Musees Natio[n-]
aux, Paris.

3. Amphora painting of footracers at the Panathenaic Games. Photograph: British Museum.

4. Domestic Scene from an amphora. Photograph: British Museum.

15. Young Athenian men being entertained by hetairai, painted on a Greek vase. Photograph: British Museum.

16. Young Athenian woman and mirror, painted on a bowl. Photograph: British Museum.

Pythoness and Goat-God

North of the Peloponnesus, in the ancient district of Phocis, a land of hilly grandeur shelving to the Gulf of Corinth, was a celebrated oracle, a source of holy wisdom, consulted by Spartan and Athenian alike. It lay beneath the peaks of Mount Parnassus in a place of wild and rustic fascination named Delphi.

Here, abutting the high range, two craggy walls formed a narrow gorge through which cascaded a clear stream, the Castalia. To the haunting beauties of this spot, nature had added a special touch. As the sun rose, its shafts struck and irradiated part of the flanking cliffs before its disk appeared above the hilltops. For this reason, they were called Phaedriades, the Gleaming Rocks. On a broad ledge deep in the valley, a temple had been raised to the sun-god, Apollo, and here came travelers from all Greece, and many lands beyond, in search of divine advice and information.

The urge to seek supernatural guidance in life's daily problems is as old as man himself. Today, when educated people are either godless or hesitate to regard God as a professional advice bureau, millions still consult fortune tellers and astrologers (if somewhat ashamedly) about personal or business matters.

The ancient Greek felt no compunction over troubling his gods for counsel on the most mundane affairs, and would almost certainly do so where important enterprise was concerned. In return, since he imagined the gods in human terms, he made what he considered a fair offering for the services rendered. Such transactions were conducted through oracles, that is, shrines where priests received and processed inquiries before giving answers inspired, it was hoped, by the gods they worshiped.

There were a number of oracular shrines in Greece of varied reputation, but none so famous or widely consulted as that of Apollo at Delphi. A constant stream of private individuals and public envoys arrived at the temple: Spartans by ship across the gulf between the Peloponnesus and Phocis, then inland from the port of Cirrha (later Itéa); Athenians through neighboring Boeotia and over the mountain range; others from the north, from as far as Thrace and Chalcidice. Kings and princes, lured by the fame of the oracle, sailed the Aegean to seek advice.

The procedure at Delphi was as follows: All visitors, having taken part in rituals of purification and sacrifice, handed their inquiries to the priests, who retired to the depths of the sanctuary. Here, a priestess, the Pythia or pythoness (supposedly possessed of the spirit of a huge serpent slain by Apollo), sat in communion with the god, for whom she would act as a medium. In preparation for her role, she had fasted, bathed in the Castalia and chewed the leaves of a sacred laurel. Her message would be delivered from the tripod, the three-legged stool of inspiration. When the influence of Apollo moved her, the priestess broke into convulsions, issuing semicoherent sounds. From these sounds the priests elucidated a response to the inquiries.

Plainly, the role of the priests in the oracular process was crucial. It gave them great influence in the affairs of ancient Greece, and posed the endless and testing challenge of upholding the oracle's reputation for being omniscient. To this end, they developed a canny tendency to present the responses of their god with a certain ambiguity, commonly in the form of a riddle which unloaded the responsibility for error on the recipient. Their shrewder patrons went to some pains to circumvent such tactics. When the Athenians once wished to know if they should build on a plot of sacred land, they sent two jars, one golden, one silver, to the Delphic oracle, the jars representing affirmative and negative. The question—By which jar should they be guided?—concealed the nature of the problem from the priests, leaving little room for a devious rejoinder. There is no doubt that the Greeks were sometimes skeptical of the interpretive capacity and integrity of the priesthood, though the validity of the divine response itself was not queried.

Overall, the influence of the Delphic oracle on Greece was vast and in many ways favorable. The central position of the temple, its endless flow of visitors from all parts of the Hellenic world, assured that its guardians were exceptionally well informed. From generation to generation, the priestly families of Delphi acquired a fund of worldly knowledge and sagacity which placed a high value on their counsel.

Much successful colonization, for example, was advised by the oracle. Before embarking for new lands, pioneers and colonists would, as a matter of course, consult the temple of Apollo. Herodotus reported it as remarkable that a Spartan adventurer, Dorieus, "neither took counsel of the oracle at Delphi as to where he should go, nor observed the customary usages." The oversight was reason enough, the scribe implies, for the failure of this man's foreign enterprise.

In matters of morality, Delphi provided an enlightened lead. Both in private dispute and state affairs, the Delphian priests maintained a fair record, despite occasional and scandalous blemishes, for exercising their detachment on the side of justice and integrity.

One conflict in which they showed themselves unremittingly partisan was the struggle to free Athens from the tyrant Hippias, the retrograde son (as has already been told) of Pisistratus.

The leaders of the struggle, a clan called the Alcmaeonids, whose chief was the great reformer Cleisthenes, took good care to cultivate the favor of the priesthood at Delphi. When the old sanctuary of Apollo was burned out by mischance, the

Alcmaeonids contracted to build a new one, installing a magnificent marble frontage at their own cost. As some had it, the Alcmaeonids bribed the Delphian priesthood. It depends on how one looks at it. If the conscience of the holy ones told them that the oppressive Hippias was bad for Athens, then inducements to act in accord with their conscience may not have seemed to their pragmatic minds inappropriate. In the sense that offerings were an essential part of the process, the oracular transaction was always a commercial one.

At all events, the priests addressed themselves to the problem of ousting the tyrant. The trouble was that neither the Alcmaeonids nor the mass of disgruntled Athenians were strong enough to overthrow the regime without assistance, while the source best equipped to render military aid, the Spartan government, had authoritarian sympathies with the Pisistratids and was reluctant to march against Hippias. Delphi put the pressure on. Whenever the Spartans consulted the oracle, either as a public body or privately, the only response they could get was: "First, free Athens from the despot."

Eventually, the pertinacity of the oracle paid off. A Spartan king named Cleomenes led an army to Athens, blockaded Hippias in the Acropolis and finally forced his expulsion from Athens.

That was in 510 B.C., two decades before Marathon. The ensuing relationship between Sparta and Athens must now become our story for a moment.

Most kings like to have their own way—they tend to be spoiled from birth—and Cleomenes was no exception. But his full exercise of power was unusual in Sparta, where kings were restricted, and he owed the fact to his prestige as a warrior. His chief exploit was the defeat of the Argives near Tiryns, thus securing Sparta's dominance over the Peloponnese. To show that he was a king to be reckoned with, he rubbed the defeat in, supposedly burning hundreds of Argives in a sacred grove. This was not the best of Spartan behavior—but it would be unwise to believe everything written about Cleomenes: he had many enemies. Nevertheless, it can be stated with safety that he was not the kind of man to relish the democratic reforms which swept Athens on the expulsion of Hippias. Indeed, he was soon regarding the new republic with a malevolence none the less bitter for having lent a hand in its troubled birth.

For their own part, the Athenians had been obliged to join the Peloponnesian league as the price of their deliverance—which gave Sparta, as its head, a certain right of interference in the affairs of Athens.

Cleomenes was not slow to assert the prerogative. Retracing his steps to Attica, he entered the city with his bodyguards in an attempt to dissolve its new constitution and set up an oligarchy. He misjudged the mood of the citizens. Rising against him, they forced him to retreat, as had Hippias earlier, to the Acropolis, where, after three days, he had to swallow his pride and capitulate.

Within months, he was plotting revenge against Athens. This time, Cleomenes persuaded two northern neighbors of the city—the Boeotians, who had old grudges to settle, and the Chalcidians, who were frankly opportunist—to strike south at the republic while Sparta and her Peloponnesian allies invaded Attica from the west. The plan, though formidable, was ill-fated.

It has been seen that there were two kings from two royal families at Sparta, and now the second king of the day, Demaratus, accompanied Cleomenes. The notion of establishing an oligarchy in place of the democracy had been dropped. Nothing less than the resurrection of a tyranny at Athens now satisfied Cleomenes. This was going a bit too far for some of his allies, who began to have second thoughts. The Corinthians, a commercially minded people, put their heads together and decided that their business interests were better suited by a buoyant rather than a suppressed Athens. Since what seems good for a man's pocket mostly suits him ideologically, the

Corinthians declared the expedition unjust and returned home. Their departure upset the Peloponnesian army. A single leader might have rallied its spirits, but too many kings, like too many cooks, may spoil the banquet, and when Cleomenes and Demaratus aired their jealousy in argument the rest of their allies followed the Corinthians. Finally, the Spartans themselves called the war off.

That left the Boeotians and the Chalcidians in the field. Neither were a match for the Athenians on their own, and they tried to join forces. The men of Athens, however, caught them beforehand and crushed them separately in two battles.

The whole affair was a rousing triumph for democratic Athens, which not only survived the attempt on its liberty but actually gained territory from the defeated northerners into the bargain. The chains in which Boeotian and Chalcidian prisoners were held until ransomed were preserved on the Acropolis, and part of the ransom used to dedicate a bronze chariot to Athene, the foremost goddess worshiped there.

According to Herodotus, whose travels introduced him to varied forms of government, and who had experienced tyranny at firsthand:

> Thus did the Athenians gain strength; and it is plain, not just from this instance but from many everywhere, that freedom is an excellent thing. While they continued under the rule of tyrants, the Athenians were no more valiant than any of their neighbours, but no sooner did they throw off the yoke than they became decidedly the first of all. These things show that, while under oppression, they let themselves be beaten, since they strove for a master; but when they got their freedom each man was eager to give the best for himself. So fared it now with the Athenians.

The Boeotians and Chalcidians were thwarted in 506. A few years later Cleomenes made a last attempt to wreck Athenian democracy.

At a congress of Peloponnesian representatives in Sparta, he put forward a project for restoring Hippias as tyrant of Athens. In a biting denunciation of the proposal, attributed to Sosicles, a Corinthian member, Herodotus reflects the mounting repugnance in Greece for autocracy:

> As soon heaven be below and the earth above, and men live in the sea while fish take their place on land, as propose to put down free governments . . . There is nothing in the whole world so unjust, nothing so bloody, as a tyranny. If you would wish to see other cities under despotic rule, begin by putting a tyrant above yourselves.

The meeting rejected the proposal, leaving Hippias, his momentarily raised hopes demolished, to pursue his intrigues with the Persians.

Cleomenes diverted part of his frustration to a bitter feud with his co-monarch Demaratus, whose deposition he eventually contrived with the aid of the Delphic oracle. Later, however, it was declared that he had bribed the Delphian authorities, and popular indignation obliged him to flee from Sparta. At length, he took his own life in a fit of madness.

Meanwhile, by the first decade of the fifth century, Athens and Sparta had established peace with each other and even some cooperation in external matters. It was against this background that Philippides urged his tired limbs through Laconia.

The Athenian messenger reached Sparta on the ninth day of Boedromion, a Greek month corresponding roughly to September, urgently seeking the ear of the ephors.

One can imagine the apprehension of Philippides. The city was *en fête*, its people engrossed in their great local festival, the Carnea, an occasion said to have been inaugurated by the musician Terpander, the founder of Greek classical music.

While the Spartan system was geared to military efficiency, the state did not spring to battle eagerly. On the contrary, some accounts see it as hesitant, even backward, in engaging its armed skills. Furthermore, though the hostile policy of Cleomenes was obsolete, few Spartans had any overwhelming compulsion to preserve the Athenian style of democracy.

On the other hand, Athens had been at least technically a member of the Spartan league since the expulsion of Hippias, and could properly expect support against foreign aggression. By and large, the Spartan, like most professional soldiers, was chivalric in upholding his pacts and obligations. Above all, there was the mutual fear of Eastern might. With a foothold in Greece itself, where would the invaders stop? If Athens fell to the Persians, could Sparta withstand the onward march of the mammoth empire of Darius?

Doubtless, Philippides put such points forcefully. "Men of Lacedaemon," Herodotus has him address the Spartans, "the Athenians pray you come to their assistance and not allow our most ancient Hellenic city to be reduced to servitude by the barbarians."

The response has been interpreted, probably unfairly, as equivocal. In short, it was a promise of armed aid with the proviso that the Carnea must be completed first. The Spartans declined to march until the festival ended at full moon, on the fifteenth—a delay of six days which might well prove disastrous for Athens.

Now, while this can be seen as an excuse to evade responsibility, there is a simpler explanation. The Carnea had profound religious implications for the Spartans. War, too, involved spiritual values, a question of sacred as well as strategic considerations. The rigidity of the Spartans in such affairs was indubitable.

Not that any explanation can have held much comfort for Philippides, duly compelled to retrace his lone journey with the bleak tidings. Once more threading the mountain passes, he had ample time to contemplate the fate of his compatriots. Perhaps the need to offset a sense of personal failure, or to spare them anguish, brought inspiration, for the story was later told that the celebrated long-distance runner arrived home in Athens with a promise of assistance altogether more encouraging than the message from Sparta. Toiling beneath the cliffs of Mount Parthenium, it seems he had fancied that the hill god Pan, a deity the Greeks visualized with horns and goat's feet, hailed him from the heights with an ultimatum: Honor Pan and Pan would succor Athens in its crisis. As a result of the tale, a shallow cave was turned into a temple for the shaggy god at the northwest corner of the Acropolis, where sacrifices were made to him.

Whatever its origin, the story would scarcely have dismayed the Persians at Marathon. Behind them, hundreds of war galleys lay on the shelving beach, backed by laden transports. The coastal plain teemed with the warriors of Darius, "lord of all men from the rising to the setting sun." Among them, resplendent in the panoply of high command, flushed by their conquering progress through the Aegean isles, strode Artaphernes, nephew of the emperor, and Datis, a general from the warlike land of Media. With them, hungry for his long-postponed revenge, was Hippias.

Twenty miles ahead, a mere jog for the hardened horsemen of the Asiatic, reclined the queen of Greek cities and all her soft pleasures. The soldiers of the empire were sanguine. A city of talkers and thinkers, of theatergoers and frequenters of symposia, where none was king and all called their many views! Such people would need more than a goat-god to save them.

Part 2
Where Empires Throve

Parthians and Medes, and Elamites, and dwellers in Mesopotamia, and in Judea, and Cappadocia, in Pontus, and Asia
. . .
—The Acts of the Apostles, ii.9

While the tiny crucible of Athens bubbled with creative genius, the great cauldron of Persia brimmed with a different brew: the fiery and addictive draught of imperialism which now overflowed the west of the empire.

Imperialism, the extension of empire, has appeared throughout history under many pretexts and many forms of government, but never more dramatically than under the Persian despots of the sixth and fifth centuries before Christ. Of these, Darius was among the greatest. Absolute master, sole fountain of authority to his people, his word was law across dominions so vast they diminished Attica to territorial insignificance. Persia itself covered more than a million square miles and almost every imaginable type of country, from towering mountains to flat, breathless deserts, from steaming jungle to fresh, fertile valleys. Beyond, the empire sprawled into Africa, the Levant, Asia Minor and India.

Susa, the administrative center of this huge realm, tucked beneath the Zagros Mountains, which shelve from modern Iran to the Iraqi frontier, was then perhaps the most cosmopolitan place on earth. Its palace was graced by the skills of Ionian stonemasons, Egyptian goldsmiths, Lydian woodworkers and Median artists, and embodied bricks from Babylonia, timber from Gandhara, gold from Sardis and Bactria, lapis lazuli from Maracanda, turquoise from Khwarezm, ivory from Sind and Arachosia. Today, such names are obscure to most of us, yet once the foremost highways of the human race led to them.

To follow the royal road west from Susa through Nineveh and Comana to the kingdoms of Asia Minor, or to take the great trails of trade and migration east around the barren wastes of the Iranian plateau to the Indus and Oxus, was like tracing the strands of some primitive necklace strung here and there with a precious stone. Set against seemingly boundless tracts of desert would appear a palmy oasis or bosky valley where sinewy nomads of the wilderness rubbed shoulders with softer denizens of farm and fragrant garden.

In far-flung markets warlike tribesmen from highland fast-nesses mingled with industrious plainsmen from the banks of broad, unhurried rivers. Everywhere the emperor's governors held sway, often backed by contingents of royal troops. Pound-ing cavalry raised the dust of distant mesas; imperial footmen slogged their way across arid routes.

Resplendent in tiara and purple robe, and upon a golden couch, the king of kings surveyed his kingdom. Persia, ex-claimed Darius, was "beautiful: full of good horses and good men." It was, of course, a selective view, but then emperors can afford to be selective. Strabo, the Greek geographer, later cor-roborated the bounties of the Persian dominions, its vines and its orchards. "Beehives are in the trees," he reported, "and the leaves flow with honey."

The royal table abounded with good things. Surrounded by cupbearers and captains, musicians and chamberlains, the em-peror picked at ostrich, goose and game flesh, sucked sticky desserts, took wine from noble goblets. Court guests were pam-pered, harem favorites were cosseted, the king's eunuchs grew fat.

It was not, however, from the larders of the land—the flocks and fruit groves—that Persia derived its dynamic growth so much as from the challenging wastes interspersing them. The need to traverse great deserts to grasp opportunities, the neces-sity to overcome drought, the incentive to adapt to fierce climates—it was these which bred resilience and mobility, stir-ring the people to visions of empire. Such visions were deep-rooted in the Persian heritage.

The earliest civilization in Persia had emerged from prehistory about 2600 B.C. at the head of the Persian Gulf which was then many miles inland of its present location. Here, between the low desert of Arabia and the bleak steppe of the Iranian plateau, two rivers, the Tigris and Euphrates, dumped their silt in a warm, marshy delta.

At first people called it simply The Land, and strange tales surrounded it. According to a tradition celebrating the role of water in this culture, the folk of The Land lived like wild beasts until an amphibious monster, half-fish, half-man, appeared on their shores to teach the blessings of farming, letters, laws, arts and sciences. For thousands of years, ran the legend, the teachings of the monster, whose name was Oannes, benefited the populace until a great disaster occurred: the disaster all people who dwell by rivers dread—a deluge.

It is during this pre-flood period that the mists of distance begin to part and historical figures replace the wraiths and prodigies. From place to place, an urban settlement, ruled by a priestly king, appears amid the winding streams. The name of The Land is now Sumer, the Shinar of the Book of Genesis, and its kingdoms include such names as Ur, Umma and Uruk.

Of these, Ur was perhaps the most powerful. A king of Ur, Meskalamdug, is the first notable of Sumer—the first Sumerian —known to us. It is impossible not to marvel at these hoary folk. The Sumerians, who spent a great deal of time fighting each other when not embroiled with racial outsiders, shaved their heads and faces, wore fringed skirts sometimes covered by long cloaks, and went to war in four-wheeled donkey chariots.

What survives of their artwork, including splendid story panels of lapis-lazuli mosaic inset with mother-of-pearl, represents the Sumerians as quaintly gnomelike creatures with odd puffin noses, and as being full of childish character—but their accomplishments suggest otherwise.

Excavations at Ur have revealed that Sumerian civilization had achieved an amazing degree of sophistication even before the deluge, in which, according to the legend of Sumer, a village headman called Ziudsuddu played the role given Noah by the Hebrews. The highly organized Sumerian settlements, built of sun-dried brick and dominated by pyramidal temples crowned by lofty shrines, housed men of no mean physique and ingenuity.

Among the great intellectual triumphs passed to later men by the Sumerians were the invention of cuneiform inscription (the earliest known form of writing), the codification of social laws, the beginnings of such sciences as astronomy and medicine (the Greeks owed a debt to them) and a time-keeping system of twelve double hours, divided into units of sixty, which survives in use to the present day.

Less is known of Sumer's time-honored enemy, Elam, a mountainous province to the east of the two rivers. Though its capital, Susa, was to become the ruling seat of Darius and the nerve-center of the great Persian empire, the Sumerians regarded it as a benighted place. To the Sumerians, Elam was the home of savage predators, a constant menace to the people of the river lands. Its hills and forests were regarded with fear and animosity.

In Sumerian legend, a great hero named Gilgames sets out to beard the king of Elam in a dense cedar grove. Helped by a female magician and a devoted monster, Gilgames creeps through the trees—whose height and thickness fill him with wonder—surprises and kills the monarch, then escapes in triumph.

Throughout the history of Sumer, in which aggression whirls from quarter to quarter with dizzying inconstancy, hostility toward the Elamites is singularly permanent. Initially Ur is dominant in Sumer, founding the first of the recorded dynasties after the great flood—or, rather, the floods, for a series of inundations swamped the lowlands. Then the dynasts of Ur are overthrown by a rival power, the house of Lagash, which, in turn, is toppled by Umma. And all the time the raiding Elamites have to be warded off.

In the second half of the third millennium, the first bold strokes of imperialism marked Persian history. The king of Umma, one Lugalzaggisi, exhilarated by his new hegemony over Sumer, decided to broaden his horizons to the west, where the sea-skirt lands of the Levant beckoned.

In a cluster of successful campaigns, he established the first Sumerian empire between the Persian Gulf and the Mediterranean. Such euphoria as Umma experienced did not last long. Lugalzaggisi had scarcely celebrated his achievement when he was faced by a new challenger for control of the land of the rivers, a northern king of formidable repute named Sargon.

Sargon was a Semite. The origins of the Semites are speculative. They first appear on the historic circuit of the Middle East in Upper Syria, from which they spread south to Palestine and east to Akkad, a region neighboring Sumer to the north. Unlike the shaven Sumerians, the Semitic Akkadians grew their locks and wore thick beards. They also spoke a different language. In their affairs, Sargon looms large, though fuzzy in outline. It was his boast that he "poured his glory upon the world," Sumer being an early and not entirely appreciative recipient. Having attained power in Akkad about 2236 B.C., he promptly upturned Lugalzaggisi and subjugated the Sumerians.

While conspiracy and insurrection demonstrated their distaste for Semitic rule, the Sumerians stood to gain some benefits. For one thing, Sargon quickly struck fear into Elam, entering Susa and devastating the lands of Sumer's old enemies. For another, he organized a regular system of communication throughout the empire, extending its influence as far as, and beyond, the Taurus Range. He also commissioned Semitic scribes to compile and translate the old laws and religious writings of the land he had occupied, storing their work in a temple at Uruk.

But Sumerian resentment of the Akkad dynasty went deep. For well over a century resistance smoldered; then both rulers and ruled were confronted by a dire threat. Exploding from highland strongholds in the far north, in Armenia and thereabouts, two groups of warlike Asiatic tribesmen, the Gutians and Lullubians, swarmed onto the plains of the great rivers and raced south.

As the Akkadians struggled to stem this tide on their frontiers, the long-frustrated Sumerians rose with a vengeance. The result was total anarchy. The savage Gutians overran the empire, settled themselves in Assyria and ravaged and plundered through Akkad into Sumer. For a hundred years or so, the Gutians mocked the refinement of centuries—an early lesson for civilization that chronological progression does not guarantee "progress."

Then, as the havoc subsided and the smoke of destruction cleared, a curious restitution took place. It was not the ruined Akkad dynasty which rose from the ashes but a clutch of new Sumerian sovereigns. First Lagash and then Uruk resurrected their glories, to be eclipsed by Ur, where a king named Urnammu founded a new dynasty, the third. The Sumerian wheel had turned full circle.

For a brief but notable period after the defeat of the last Gutian king in 2023 B.C., Ur throbbed with new power and authority. The Semitic language was dropped from the texts and Sumerian returned to official use. Not just Sumer and Akkad, but that traditional thorn in the side, the land of Elam, fell under the hegemony of the brilliantly recovered Ur of the third dynasty. For the first time ever, a major part of Elam, including Susa, was subjected to permanent administration by Sumerians. Laborers were recruited there for building projects; native chiefs were replaced by officials from Sumer—one district of Elam was even ruled by the daughter of a king of Ur.

In a strenuous bid to unify the empire, Urnammu and his successors constructed roads and canals, dispatched investigators to all points to check that their orders were carried out, and maintained a substantial police force to keep the peace. Since it all cost a lot of money, each city was obliged to contribute according to its size and wealth. Moreover, the priests who ran the treasury—the priests ran many things in Sumer—made loans of cash and cattle to the king's subjects from which the royal coffers drew interest.

Excavations in modern times have revealed numerous records of such transactions, inscribed on tablets of baked clay by the clerks of the treasury and endorsed by auditors. The observation that a systematic bookkeeping operation, highly staffed and headed by accountants of priestly station, was central to a civilization two thousand years before Christ may not be a particularly romantic one, but it certainly bridges the centuries with a sense of familiarity.

Yet, for all its industry and aptitude, the third dynasty of Ur was ephemeral. At home, Semitization had gained too deep a hold to be exorcised; abroad, the Lullubians and their cousins the Simurrians replaced the defeated Gutians as a savage threat. While the Lullubians raided from the north, a Semitic people, the Amorites (the Biblical predecessors of the Israelites in Canaan), appeared aggressively from the west. When the Sumerians built a great wall to repel them, the Amorites teemed over it to wreak terror and confusion. Finally, an older foe, Elam, delivered the mortal blow. For decades, Elamite insurgents had struggled to rid their land of rule by Sumer. At the dawn of the second millennium they succeeded. With the Sumerians again reduced to anarchy, the Elamites swept vengefully to Ur itself, seized the last of its kings, one Ibi-sin, and carried him captive to Elam. Sumer never recovered its glory.

The prologue was over: the Persian drama was about to start in earnest.

10 Mother of Harlots

If Darius knew little about the Sumerian empire, whose last moments were far removed from his own day, he unquestionably knew a great deal about its fabulous inheritor, Babylon. For the fame of Babylon, a fledgling city in the time of Sargon, had soared across the ages like a great bird, gripping the imagination of the ancient world. From the seventeenth century B.C. to as late as the Christian era, Babylon was the center of western Asia, unequaled for its grandeur and influence—and the deprecations it received from some quarters.

Darius had good cause to know Babylon. Once, when the city defied him in armed revolt, he may even have anticipated the Book of Revelations: "Babylon . . . mother of harlots and abominations of the earth"! Others preferred the epithet Babylon the great.

Conquering the rebels two decades before Marathon, Darius was able to admire the mighty citadel and its surroundings for the first time as emperor: to marvel at its daunting walls, its fine palaces, its fabled "hanging gardens," the great processional way to the splendid Gate of Ishtar, its lofty temples and the towering shrine to Marduk, the exalted god.

Babylon was among the proudest possessions of the king of kings. It stood beside the Euphrates at a point (just north of the modern town of Hilla) where the Tigris nudged toward its sister river, forming a narrow waist of enclosed ground. Downstream lay the wider delta lands and the Persian Gulf; upstream, the broad plains of Assyria. It was the command of the middle region, the natural passage between north and south, which made Babylon queen of the river lands.

Her imposing reign brims with untold dramas, a few of which would fill an entire book. A brief summary must start with the fall of the house of Ur. At this stage, the Semitic cause came to the fore again, but the land was divided and many parts struggled for supremacy, among them the formerly unpretentious Babylon, now headed by ambitious Amorites. Long, fierce and shaded by changing alliances, the strife finally resolved in a straight issue between Larsa, ruled by a family of Elamite origin, and the Amorite dynasty of Babylon. Babylon won the fight. In 1683 B.C., the most illustrious of its early kings, Hammurabi, drove the last of his rivals from Larsa, and the land of two rivers once more paid service to a single crown. Henceforward, the old regions of Sumer and Akkad may be termed Babylonia, which stretched loosely north between the great streams.

The prospect of law, order and unity must have been widely welcomed by people weary of so much local conflict and chaos. Hammurabi, a strong soldier with a penchant for the detail of administration, was just the man to organize such attributes. Not only did he keep his governors on their toes, but he compiled a famous schedule of laws to which all could look for guidance. This compilation, undiscovered by modern scholars until the present century, is called the Code of Hammurabi. It is one of the outstanding documents of ancient history.

Owing much to Sumerian precedent, Hammurabi's code provided a basis for justice and lawful conduct throughout the dominions of Babylon which was influential for at least fifteen hundred years. Of course, it had its crudities, for barbarism was still naked in some facets of jurisprudence, but it was a tremendous advance on tribal custom in general, and evidently struck Hammurabi as a sound foundation for his professed aims of protecting the weak and making "men's flesh content."

A few of the code's abundant features may serve as example:

It required that all courts of law be strictly supervised and appeal allowed to the king, the pure source of justice. Many bad customs once prevalent—the blood feud, private retribution, marriage by capture—were no longer recognized.

It provided detailed rules for the buying, selling, letting and renting of land and property; the cultivation, grazing and irrigation of farmland; the procedures for caravan traffic and trading, loans and debt collection, shipbuilding and navigation, warehousing, the sale of intoxicants, and a host of other things.

It elaborated the rights, as well as the obligations, of people of various stations. For instance, the numerous slaves of Babylon, though head-marked for ready identification and subject to stiff penalties for desertion, were entitled to marry into the free class, in which case the offspring were then free.

The status of women received a fair share of attention.

Every lawful marriage involved a contract, and the consequences of repudiation by either party were clearly fixed.

A husband was entitled to divorce his wife at will, but he had then to restore her dowry, give her custody of the children and provide alimony—unless she had been a bad wife, in which case he might keep the dowry and the children.

For her own part, a wife might sue her husband for cruelty or neglect.

By contrast to the free and exuberant sexual ethos of early Greece, the Babylonians hedged sexual relationships with strict rules which, though roughly just between partners, presaged the prohibitive, punitive attitudes so widespread at later times.

Adultery was normally punished by drowning the guilty pair, though the code allowed that an aggrieved husband could pardon his erring wife.

The penalty for slandering a married woman was branding. Should she invite disapproval by her own extravagant behavior, she risked a sentence of enslavement.

Upon her husband's death, the wife took his place at the head of the household, sharing his estate with the children when they came of age.

In this scheme for connubial life, one inequality was glaring. And, as in most rigid sexual codes, it favored the male partner. A man might take a second and socially inferior wife, a concubine. A married woman, on the other hand, was entitled to only one husband.

Nevertheless, if at times disagreeable, the code was rational in most matters, and its descent to primitive levels was confined largely to the criminal sections.

The general principle of criminal law under Hammurabi was the *talio*, that is, retaliation in kind or by emotional association. Thus, the hand that struck a father might be cut off; the eye that gazed upon forbidden things, gouged out; the man responsible for the death of another's child, sentenced to have a child of his own killed.

Death was a common penalty for thieves and those who neglected professional duties.

The code also sanctioned trial by ordeal to settle awkward legal issues, a man's guilt or innocence depending on whether he sank or floated when fettered and tossed in the river. In considering such savageries, however, it should be remembered that trial by ordeal conducted by Christian priests was going strong in medieval Europe, twenty-five hundred years and more after Hammurabi, and that thieves were still being hanged in England a few score years ago.

In total, the code reflects the nature of a highly organized society. Such state officials as judges, tax collectors and government inspectors proliferated in the capital and provinces; merchants formed companies and opened branch offices; banking developed; an army of scribes worked on state and private documents; there was a regular postal system. All this stemmed from the roots of Sumerian genius.

The rise of Babylon itself, as has been seen, resulted from three things: its geographical situation; political circumstances which encouraged independence; and strong leadership which made the most of it.

A further factor extended Babylonian influence. From the earliest days of the river lands, religion had been inseparable from the growth and prestige of their cities. Kings were held to obtain their authority from the gods. The first kings had been priests, and the priesthood, having conceived power, had clung to it.

The Babylonians worshiped a solar deity, Marduk, who was
held to have been sired by one Enki, the water-god. Originally,
Marduk's importance was limited, but the upsurge of Babylon
promoted him—likewise the city priests—to preeminence in
the spiritual life of the empire. Usurping the powers once
attributed to older deities, Marduk became not just the son of
an exalted father but the champion of all gods and creator of
the universe.

Each year an elaborate festival was held at Babylon, including a pantomimed reenactment of the supposed struggle between the divines and the dragons of chaos, to celebrate the
making of the world by Marduk. At this function the king
suffered symbolic humiliation by being ceremonially stripped
of rank by the high priest before receiving anew his scepter by
Marduk's authority.

So firmly established became the belief in Marduk as the
heavenly source of regal power that some of the greatest kings
of western Asia—rulers under no political obligation to Babylon—traveled to the festival to renew their royal warrants.
Thus, even when secular power passed from the city, as it did
more than once in its long career, spiritual power upheld its
prestige.

The initial supremacy of Babylon, for all its administrative
energy, did not last more than half a century. In due course,
the might of Hammurabi eluding his successors, old rivalries
flared and the provinces crackled with dissension. In the far
south the Chaldeans of Sumer went so far as to create a new
royal house, the so-called second Babylonian dynasty.

Divided, the empire beckoned fresh enemies.

The Indo-European migrations and their role in Greek history have already been noted. Now, for the first time,
Mesopotamian civilization felt the repercussions of these human tides, these restless packs of fierce, nomadic warriors with
their hardy women and travel-inured brats.

Toward 1760 B.C., a people called the Hittites became prominent in Cappadocia, an easterly part of Asia Minor. The Hittite leaders were Indo-Europeans. Subjecting the natives, absorbing many in their own tribes, the Hittites began looking for new regions of expansion. From the Semitic traders based in Cappadocia, they must have heard of the well-stocked Babylonian cities to the southeast.

Suddenly, a Hittite king named Murshilish raised dust on the Babylonian horizon. From the dust emerged a rampaging tribal army. Spurring this ferocious and motley horde across the valley of the Euphrates, Murshilish burst upon Babylon, butchering and plundering. His appears to have been a crude piratical adventure, for the Hittites departed as suddenly as they had come. But, by sacking the city and toppling the last of Hammurabi's line, they had cleared the way for a more persistent invader from the easterly highlands of Zagros.

The inheritors of ravaged Babylon were the Kassites, a rugged people first mentioned in the early texts of the Elamites, with whom they variously fought and forged alliances. One Kassite incursion had already been repulsed by a son of Hammurabi, but the aggressors had settled on his northern frontiers, where their princes ruled simultaneously with the last kings of the first Babylonian dynasty.

Now, with that dominion disrupted and leaderless, the combative Kassites were well placed to take charge of its vacant throne. They did so with alacrity.

Like the Hittite rulers, the Kassite kings were of Indo-European stock, but settlement had mellowed them and they were prudent enough to ingratiate themselves with the Babylonian priesthood. Making liberal gifts to the gods and temples, they diplomatically affirmed their devotion in the language of the country. One king, Agum II, enhanced his popularity by recovering plundered statues of Marduk and his divine consort, Sarpanit, from the Hittites and restoring them to Babylon.

Indeed, the secure hold these monarchs soon established over the Babylonians suggests a rule of canny efficiency. Intellectually, they were not inspired. The third, or Kassite, dynasty of Babylonia, is not renowned for innovation. Its two most familiar contributions to Persian history were the horse, previously unknown on the river lands, and the boundary stones set up to mark gifts of land to royal favorites. But its kings had the wit to preserve what had gone before. They did so, as it happened, for close on six hundred years.

The Wrath of Nineveh

No empire on earth had equaled that of Darius and his immediate predecessors, but one earlier empire had hinted broadly at things to come, and that was the creation of Assyria, a kingdom north of Babylon crowned by the mountains of Kurdistan. At its height, the Assyrian empire, overwhelming Kassite Babylonia, ranged from the western edge of the Iranian plateau to Egypt and the Levant, a rousing example for the Persian emperors.

The empire was the result of much hard and ruthlessly efficient soldiering. Indeed, independent Assyria was founded on militarism, and its later kings relied heavily on mobile, well-organized armies. Chariots, now horse-drawn and of the two-wheeled variety, were used effectively, as was cavalry, while the increasingly important art of attacking walled cities was tackled with diligence. As time passed, the Assyrians employed carriage-mounted battering rams, siege shelters, scaling ladders, ramps, and a corps of engineers skilled in mining fortresses. Pontoon bridges were devised for river crossings.

Fighting was a way of life. "I drew the bow, sped the arrow, the mark of the warrior. I flung the quivering javelins," wrote an Assyrian monarch of his youthful education. War gods were prominent in the religion of the nation; panoramic bas-reliefs of expeditions and battle scenes, realistically modeled and detailed in armor and weaponry, ornamented its palaces. Confidently its legions marched to reduce the world.

Behind this reliance on force lay a certain disdain for diplomacy. So good did the Assyrians become at coercion, at frightening people, that they came to depend on it. Unlike the Kassites, they seldom ruled without provoking resentment and

81

discontent. Opposition was crushed with methodical brutality. When death, destruction and torture incited defiant resistance, it was met with the deportation of entire populations or with policies verging on genocide.

Finally, so great and universal was the hatred of Assyria that when its generals momentarily faltered, its power was swept away in a flash-tide of vengeance.

Assyria, the land of Assur, was originally the territory surrounding a city of that name on the Tigris, high above Babylon, at the northern extremity of the river plain. Assur is first mentioned in a letter of Hammurabi's time, when it seems to have been part of the Babylonian dominions. Later the capital was established upstream at Nineveh, and here the greatest of its rulers presided.

The most famed of Assyria's kings is Assurbanipal. Like many famous men, he was not unduly modest. Assurbanipal would have been delighted had he known that a glowing commendation of his merits would still be in circulation when men visited the moon. (To complain that he wrote it himself seems ungracious.) From rare and vivid portraits which survive of him in low-relief, Assurbanipal looks out with a serene eye—a fatherly figure with long beard and flowing locks whose somewhat professorial features add substance to his own blurb:

> Marduk, the wise one of the gods, presented me with information and understanding as a gift . . . in heavenly and earthly buildings I read and pondered, in the meetings of clerks I was present, I watched the omens, I explained the heavens with the learned priests, recited the complex multiplications and divisions not immediately apparent.
>
> I took pleasure in reproducing the beautiful Sumerian writings, which are obscure, and those of Akkad, that are difficult
> . . .
> I had the learning that all clerks possess in their maturity. At

the same time, I learned what is proper for lordship. I went my royal ways."

An unlikely reference, perhaps, from a destroyer of cities and butcher of their inhabitants, yet it must not be supposed that the Assyrians, for all their barbarity toward those who thwarted them, were uncivilized. Assurbanipal's self-tribute is not that of a man who despised the intellect. Indeed, he was a keen student, especially of archaeology and ancient literature. Modern knowledge is indebted to the avidity with which he sought and preserved the ancient texts of Sumer and elsewhere. His vast library survives to the present day.

A notable feature of Assyrian culture, at its peak, was its highly cosmopolitan nature. In it can be found not only the influence of Babylon but of such other conquered peoples as the Egyptians and Arameans. Egyptian prisoners brought many customs and objects of their own land to the cities of Assyria. The Arameans introduced their most significant product, the Aramaic alphabet, which superseded the older cuneiform writing in some instances. Again, marriages between the governing Assyrians and the nobility of dependent neighbors promoted cultural exchanges.

In short, the Assyrian empire did a great deal to encourage a uniform level of civilization in western Asia and to spread the germ of certain manners and attitudes which, in time, would be thought of as "oriental."

Except for the high-born and the prostitutes who served the armies, women became increasingly secluded and subservient, now closely veiled and closeted.

At one end of the scale, the elaborate ceremonial which grew around the kings as their power burgeoned—the scheming viziers, the hawkish war captains (turtans), the intrigue-prone harem—formed a recognizable prototype of the classic oriental court. At the other, a great mass of people grew poorer. The wholesale influx of captives from conquered lands, swelling the pool of unpaid labor, brought ruin to more and more humble freemen, thus directly and indirectly increasing the slave population, for the bankrupt freeman had no option but to sell himself into slavery.

Appeal to the king, a traditional right in the old Babylonia, became largely impractical. Not only was he geographically remote from vast numbers of his subjects, but an expanding administration bred jealous executives to block access to the source of their new power. As a result, provincial discontent, too often treated with the old violent remedies, tended to be suppressed rather than banished.

Even Assurbanipal's own brother, the governor of Babylon, defected and had to be dealt with by armed force. Sennacherib, Sargon's successor, had taken revenge on the rebellious city by sacking it and turning a canal onto the ruins, and now Assurbanipal gave his punitive column a free hand—once more, the people of Babylon were savaged and killed, their rebuilt homes destroyed.

At the same time, the king bestirred himself to put an end to the continuing independence of Elam, whose tribesmen persisted in raiding his frontiers. The moment was opportune. A palace upheaval in Susa, producing a new ruler of Elam, King Teumman, had driven a group of disgruntled princes into exile. They turned up in Assyria seeking Assurbanipal's aid to oust their rival.

The grim sequel proceeded in three acts. The first, a bloody battle at Tulliz, near Susa, was a disaster for Teumman at the hands of the Assyrian army. Attacked before they had fully assembled, the Elamites were routed, with their king hurled from his chariot as he fled the field. His head was cut off and sent to Nineveh, to be displayed at a celebration banquet. The adherents of the exiled princes now seized power in Susa, and with an Assyrian puppet installed there, the imperial troops retired.

But Elam was far from pacified, and Act Two saw daggers drawn in the capital. In a swift sequence of conspiracy and murder, enacted by a cast whose names are more impressive than their actions, Assurbanipal's puppet, one Khumban-igash, was slain by his brother, Tammaritu, who was driven from the throne by a powerful feudatory called Indabugash. Indabugash, in turn, was murdered and replaced by Khumban-Khaldash, a champion of the Elamite nobility.

Meanwhile, Tammaritu had found his way to Nineveh. At first, Assurbanipal took steps to help Tammaritu eject Khumban-Khaldash and resume the crown of Elam, but he changed his tactics on discovering that his new protégé was rashly plotting a double cross: the Elamites, having aided the latest Babylonian rising, were sheltering a party of the defeated rebels. Assurbanipal packed the untrustworthy Tammaritu back to Susa with the unenviable task of demanding their surrender. It was a vain one, for the Elamites were in no mind to betray their allies, nor was Khumban-Khaldash inclined to accommodate the man who had tried to displace him.

The scene was set for the last act. About 640 B.C., Assurbanipal, impatient of bargaining, turned loose the full armed might of Assyria on Elam with the authority to devastate the country. After sacking fourteen outlying communities, it broke into Susa, butchering, raping and pillaging. The booty was plentiful. Though Elam lacked the talent and resources of Babylonia, its people had gained much in wealth and craft from their neighbors. In the making of jewelry, they excelled the Babylonians. Moreover, their coffers were stacked with valuables looted from Akkad and Sumer. Among other prizes, thirty-two statues of Elamite monarchs in gold, silver, bronze and marble, were seized by the Assyrians. Temples were ransacked. Even the tombs of ancient heroes were broken open and their contents filched.

For those Elamites who failed to escape to the hills there was a dreadful fate. The rank and file were beaten to death, and the captains flayed alive. Finally, with Susa in ashes, the land was sown with salt to render it infertile.

Assurbanipal was satisfied. Harnessing the captured Khum-ban-Khaldash and the miserable Tammaritu to his chariot, he rode to the temple of Ishtar, the mother of heaven, to give praise. Elam was obliterated. Such was the wrath of Nineveh.

The Prophet 12

It is time to move up from the low-lying plains which produced
Ur, Babylon and Nineveh, traverse the mountainous haunts of
the Kassites and Elamites, and discover the final ethnic layer
in the pedestal from which Darius surveyed the world.

Across the Zagros Range from the populous river lands,
great waterless tracts of wilderness had limited occupation of
the Iranian plateau. Nevertheless, parts of the plateau offered
refuge and livelihood for resilient, adaptable people, and some
of the early folk wanderers had preferred to settle here rather
than fight the organized city dwellers for richer lands. Among
these migrants were two groups, the Medes and the Persians,
who belonged to a broader collection of people known as Aryans.

The Aryans, who belonged to the Indo-European family,
trundled their rude wagons onto the Iranian plateau when the
first of the Mesopotamian city civilizations were in full glory.
The newcomers were rough men, ignorant of writing, still
taking their brides by capture, living almost as simply as the
sturdy horses and scavenging flocks of cattle, sheep and goats
they brought with them.

The Medes settled in the northwest, separated by the mountains from Assyria; the Persians were to their south, on the land
to the east of the Persian Gulf where one frontier made tenuous contact with the Elamites.

For hundreds of years the Aryans made no impact on the
outer world; they were intent on tilling their plots and tending
their cattle, goading a humble living from a moody environ-
ment. Periodically the loosely organized clans might unite in
defense against raiding hillsmen or the tribes of the northern

87

steppes. Periodically an Assyrian army would cross the mountains from the west and overwhelm the scattered villages.

No Aryan leader appeared to transcend the petty chiefs and give these people the strength of national unity. For a millennium or more, they were a force unharnessed. When a general arrived to exploit their vigor and hardihood, they would rise from their stony allotments and march where he beckoned. But by the time of the accession of Assurbanipal that general had not appeared.

Nor, as it happened, was the first compelling figure in Iranian history a soldier at all, but a prophet—a prophet not of man's triumph over man but of the triumph of good over evil; a prophet whose only war was the war in the human soul.

Zarathustra (or Zoroaster, as he is better known from the Latin) had no dreams of leading Iran to great military victories, but when the kings and emperors departed, it would be his simple message rather than their grandiose achievements which would live on in human consciousness.

Zoroaster is sometimes called a Mede, sometimes a Persian, sometimes a Bactrian, while his birth is disputed between about 1000 and 660 B.C. More certainly, he was born of an earthy, pastoral people, at heart a peasant farmer for whom agriculture and cattle-breeding were the commended callings of an Aryan.

Thus the ideal life in the eyes of a Zoroastrian was a natural one: "It is where one of the faithful makes a home with cattle, wife and children, and where the cattle thrive and the dog, the wife, the child, the fire are thriving . . . where the faithful one cultivates corn, grass and fruit in good measure; where he irrigates dry ground and drains ground that is too wet." Productive animals were cherished—"the gift of a pair of fowls to the faithful is as the gift of a house with a hundred columns"—and the dog acknowledged as a valued friend: "For no home could subsist on God's earth but for those two dogs, the shepherd's dog and the house dog."

There is a note of wholesome sanity in the outlook of Zoroaster which contrasts with, for example, the superstitious sacrifices common to his own day, or, for that matter, the insensible abuses of land and livestock in modern times.

Not that his was merely a rustic philosophy. On top of this simple view of the good life, Zoroaster proclaimed a spiritual vision of such profundity that its echoes have been resounding in the religious faith of countless millions ever since.

Briefly, the prophet rejected polytheism, the worship of many gods, in favor of a single god he called Ahura Mazda (later Ormazd), the Wise Lord. It was, perhaps, less a name to the prophet than the definition of a force. At least, it was the content rather than the image of Zoroaster's divinity which set it apart from the run of gods. As the prophet saw it, Ahura Mazda was the embodiment of all divine character, of truth, of righteousness, purity, light and life. To the Wise Lord belonged the good among men, the beneficent among animals, the nourishing among plants and vegetables.

Since it was Mazda's purpose, and the duty of the faithful, to extend this benign domain, Zoroaster held out certain inducements. The man who chose the true faith might expect to prosper. In an immortal life beyond the grave, all would receive their just deserts. But there was more to earning eternal bliss than lip service, for the crucial point about Zoroaster's god was that he was a moral divinity, making ethical demands on his worshipers. The ethics were vague. Zoroaster was no Greek philosopher, nor were the people to whom he preached a city intelligentsia. Nevertheless the objective was clear enough—the ultimate triumph of the benign over the malevolent in an all-embracing kingdom of god in heaven and on earth. Without doubt, it was a vision of singular novelty among a populace ridden with the fear of devils, the arbitrary demands and retributions of a pack of gods, the uninviting prospect of death itself, often a violent one.

Indeed, for the priests who at length presumed to take

charge of it, Zoroaster's doctrine was altogether too abstract and negligent of worldly trappings. While prophets tend to look out through clear windows, priests have commonly had a preference for stained glass—it may obscure the view, but it throws glorious colors on their own role. Hence, much of the paraphernalia of the past was duly revived and stuck onto the pure teaching: sacrifices, elaborate purification ceremonies, all kinds of superfluous ritual, together with such shades of primitive worship as fire altars and fire temples. Many of the old gods and devils were invoked, now in the lesser parts of good or evil genii, to provide a bumper supporting cast.

Finally, with Zoroaster committed to legend, the priesthood was itself taken over and protected by kings and princes for whom the striking popularity of Mazda opened new vistas of authority. Surrounded by their conquering war captains and glittering treasures, the mighty emperors of Persia would bow before the Wise Lord in ostentatious and, who knows, probably sincere obeisance to the vision of a man who was loath to see a beast killed, and who reckoned wealth in a peasant's plot.

Of all the people of the Iranian plateau, it was the Medes, closest to Assyria, whose introduction to civilization was the least agreeable. Again and again, they made easy sport for the western kings. Campaigning in Media was relatively safe and very profitable. It kept the Assyrian armies out of mischief when there were no great wars elsewhere, and it could be relied upon to produce droves of slaves and cattle from the backward and uncohesive Aryans. Among other things, Media was widely noted for a breed of dun and gray horses which grazed there, the so-called Nisaean horses. Renowned for speed and endurance, they were a particular target for the Assyrians, who swept whole areas of the plateau bare of man and beast.

At last, the victims had had enough. "We cannot possibly, they said, go on living in this country if things continue like this; let us elect a king so the land may be justly governed." So

Herodotus, recounting Aryan legend, wrote of the eventual decision of the Medes to place their clans under a common chief, to seek strength through unity.

The first king, it seems, was a certain Dayaukku, or Deiokes, a headman noted in the villages for his justice. He made his capital in the shadow of Mount Alvand, the classical Orontes, at the eastern end of the pass which linked the plateau with the river lands, and it became known as Ecbatana, or Hamadan. Here, according to Herodotus, rose a city of many-colored walls and gilded battlements, plainly inspired by Babylonia, and a court evolved on the style of the Assyrian emperors. Deiokes welded the clans into a kingdom. His son, Phraortes, absorbed the kindred tribes of the Persians in the dominion. But it was their successor, Huvakshatara, better known as Cyaxares, for whom Iranian history had been waiting.

In Cyaxares the Aryans at last had their general. He inspected his forces. The material was good—hard men inured to toil and the elements, embittered by centuries of suffering at the hands of the western foe—but it needed reorganizing. Cyaxares replaced the tribal levies of old with a regular army on the lines of the Assyrians. He armed his footmen well with bow, sword and javelin. He built a strong body of cavalry from the inveterate horsemen of the plateau, braves accustomed from childhood to ride rough and shoot from horseback. And he seasoned his forces in a long and fierce struggle against a wild northern enemy, the marauding Scythians from the Russian steppes.

With the Scythians beaten, Cyaxares turned west. The moment had come for a grim revenge.

13 Chariots Shall Rage

"And it shall come to pass that all they that look upon thee shall flee from thee, and say, Nineveh is laid waste: who will bemoan her?" So the oracle of the Israeli god, Yawheh, according to Nahum, the Old Testament prophet. "Woe to the bloody city!"

And it came to pass.

In 626 B.C. Assurbanipal died and a shiver of vengeful anticipation thrilled the empire. From the Mediterranean to the Zagros Mountains, rebellion stirred. The governor of Babylon, Nabopolassar, threw off his allegiance to Assyria, declared a new Babylonian dynasty and took up arms. The whole of lower Mesopotamia followed him. Not to be outdone, Egypt reasserted its martial potential. Advancing through Palestine, Necho II, the Egyptian monarch, fell on Josiah, King of Judah, at Megiddo. The gory field of Armageddon betokened the rousing of the Pharaohs.

With the empire in tumult, Cyaxares delivered the fatal blow. Sweeping from the plateau, his cavalry and charioteers devastated the heartlands of Assyria, investing Nineveh. Assurbanipal's successors fought desperately. The conflict was recounted vividly by Nahum: "The noise of a whip, and the noise of the rattling of the wheels, and of the prancing horses, and of the jumping chariots. The horseman lifteth up both the bright sword and the glittering spear: and there is a multitude of slain, and a great number of carcasses; and there is no end of their corpses; they stumble upon their corpses."

The Biblical adage about violence destroying the violent was grimly true of Assyria. In the final attack, Cyaxares led the allied forces of Media and Babylonia against the doomed capital. Its besieged monarch, having resisted to the last moment, caused himself and his family to be incinerated rather than face the tender mercies of the enemy.

Woe, indeed, Nineveh! "The chariots shall rage in the streets, they shall jostle one against another in the broad ways: they shall seem like torches, they shall run like lightnings . . . The gates of the rivers shall be opened, and the palace shall be dissolved."

It was 606 B.C. or thereabouts. A few short years had passed since the glory of Assurbanipal. In those few years the mightiest empire then known had collapsed like a pack of cards.

One result of the breakup of empire is that resentment hitherto directed by its parts toward the dominant state is free to find new outlets. While the lion rules the feast, lesser beasts may commiserate, but when the lion departs their competitive instincts reassert themselves. Such was the case on the demise of Assyria. Necho of Egypt had grabbed Palestine and Syria while Nineveh was in its death throes. Babylon, bristling with fresh vitality under Nabopolassar and his successor, Nebuchadnezzar, took the rich river lands. Cyaxares held sway in the uplands, adding Armenia to Persia and Media, and looking west to Cappadocia.

It was unlikely that these ambitious men would be content with the status quo, and when Necho, inflated by the revival of Egyptian fortunes, turned up on the Euphrates with his army, Nebuchadnezzar prepared for a trial of strength.

The battle took place at Carchemish, west of the river, and though the Egyptians were reinforced by Ethiopians, Libyans and even a band of Greek mercenaries, the Babylonians triumphed. While Necho retreated to Egypt, Nebuchadnezzar overthrew the government which that king had forced on Judah, took Jerusalem and led part of its population in captivity to Babylon. Astir with new trade and construction projects, the cities of Babylonia assumed unprecedented splendor and magnificence.

Meanwhile, Cyaxares concentrated his efforts in the northern highlands, pushing steadily west into Asia Minor. The tribes in his path had been left exhausted and confused by savage Scythian incursions and by the depredations of another marauding people, the Cimmerians, who had rampaged through the lands of the Black Sea. It was not difficult for organized troops to subdue them, and the Medes marched on until they reached the river Halys.

The ruddy stream was a significant frontier. Ahead lay a world little known to them save through travelers' gossip—the Greek world of the Aegean. Its nearest outposts were the coastal colonies of Ionia, unfamiliar cities of fair climate, full of alien people, reputedly quick-witted and capable, versed in the arts of navigation, commerce, painting, literature and rhapsody. But if these filled the Iranian mind with curiosity, a more immediately intriguing prospect confronted Cyaxares: Lydia.

Lydia, the land between the Halys and the Ionian seaboard, was renowned for its richness. It was, indeed, exceedingly fertile. The hillsides were swathed in fir and vine; the plains produced heavy crops of corn and saffron; the capital, Sardis, was said to bestride a river of golden sand. Fecundity was impressed on its psychology. Lydian girls gained their dowries by sacred prostitution in devotion of the mother goddess, Cybele, while huge phallic emblems in stone were raised to ward off evil.

For the Greeks, Lydia was a land of luxury and a source of exotic mythology. Homer gave it as the domain of the Amazons, a race of female warriors who disdained to habitate with the male sex. Amazonian legend was powerful and long-lived. These creatures of fantasy were considered a severe test for the heroes of Greek myth. According to one belief, they dispensed with their right breasts the better to exercise their sword-arms, and since an exclusively feminine race raised problems of procreation, it was held that they mated with visiting foreigners and banished their sons at an early age. Probably, the legend arose from the rituals of Lydian priestesses, who danced with bows and shields in honor of Cybele.

At all events, the Lydians did not lack enterprise. In trade and art they formed a discerning link between Greece and Asia Minor. They are the first people known to have used coinage, and they have been credited with the invention of many games, including dice, and the innovation of wayside hostelries for travelers.

Civilized and prosperous, they also had a tough streak. For decades they defended their homes stubbornly against the Cimmerians, until an outstanding Lydian monarch, Alyattes, fourth of the so-called Mermnad dynasts, routed the marauders.

Alyattes, who reigned for no less than fifty-seven years, established Lydian dominance over the whole of Asia Minor west of the Halys, not excluding the Greek cities of Ionia which, though retaining their own governments, paid taxes and other dues to Sardis. From these tributes, plus the proceeds of commerce, Alyattes amassed the treasure which was to make the name of his successsor, Croesus, synonymous with massive wealth. It enabled the Lydian monarch to hire Greek troops and maintain an elite cavalry of high reputation. In all, Alyattes was a ruler to be reckoned with, and it was Alyattes whom Cyaxares faced across the Halys.

That the Mede should have marched so far to resist the temptations of Lydia was a tale for the credulous. Conflict was inevitable. The cause traditionally assigned to it—it is, perhaps, a mark of grace in mankind that it tends to find naked ambition unpalatable—is bizarrely spiced. It was said that Cyaxares took a band of Scythians on the campaign as huntsmen, in whose charge he placed a number of his noble youths that they might gain experience in fieldcraft. One day the Scythians returned to camp empty-handed, whereupon the king was so abusive that they resolved to avenge themselves. The next time Cyaxares called for a banquet, they served up an abundance of somewhat suspicious meat. Then, before the king discovered that one of the young nobles was missing and could reach the distasteful conclusion that the diners had eaten him, the huntsmen fled to the Lydian court, where Alyattes declined to give them up.

Six years of war followed without a decisive stroke. The Medes were numerous and fierce in their endeavors, but they were a long way from base, and not even their own hardy horsemen could best the crack cavalry of Lydia.

Hostilities ended on a note as odd, in its way, as that which, allegedly, had provoked the war. In 585 B.C. the fighting was interrupted by a total eclipse of the sun, an omen so impressing the ranks of both armies that they displayed considerable reluctance to meet again. At this auspicious moment, Babylon stepped in to mediate, and a treaty was arranged fixing the Halys as a peace line and resulting in the diplomatic marriage of the heir apparent of Lydia to a daughter of Cyaxares.

When Cyaxares died a year later, his successor, Ishtuvegu, or Astyages, inherited a period of uncommon tranquillity. He made the most of it. Amid the red and purple robes, the gold chains and collars, the rarefied sport and ceremonial of the Assyrian-style court at Ecbatana, Astyages cultivated what seems to have been a middling talent for voluptuous idleness. Leisurely days were passed in set-piece hunts at the game park, or "paradise," of the capital; languorous nights with his palace concubines. It was a novel life for an Aryan, even a nobleman, and one which may well have offended people accustomed to the vigorous, earthy travail commended by Zoroaster.

In any case, there was no great rush to support him when, in 550 B.C., a Persian rebellion put an end to his regime, placing the erstwhile junior partners of western Iran on the high throne.

The new ruler—the founder of Persian power—was named Kurush (Latinized as Cyrus), and his stature is acknowledged by the inventiveness expended on his origins. In one account, he is seen as the son of Astyages's daughter, Mandane, who has been married to a nondescript Persian noble in order that her

husband shall not rival the Median king. Following a premoni-
tion that her offspring will overpower all Asia, Astyages orders
the infant to be exposed in the mountains, but the babe is
suckled by a dog and, later, tutored by a shepherd. This legend
combines a belief, popular in ancient times, that abandoned
infants might be reared by animals—Romulus and Remus are
well-known examples—with a handy legitimization of Persian
rule through the family of Astyages.

A second story, which Herodotus elaborates, modifies the
first by exchanging the dog for the shepherd's wife. Astyages
now entrusts the killing of the child Cyrus to a kinsman named
Harpagus, who, repelled by his squalid task, hands the infant
to the peasant woman and returns to court with her own
stillborn child as proof of the slaying. Here the revulsion to
Astyages by his own kind is implicit. Harpagus was a Median
general who rose to high favor with Cyrus.

In a different genre, Cyrus is portrayed as the son of a
nomadic bandit. After becoming the servant and protégé of
Astyages, he is inspired to rebellion by the prophecy of a
fortune teller. Another version of this plot draws from the
shepherd tale to make him the son of an honest rustic.

Against all this romance, the truth seems a bit flat. According to Cyrus himself, he was quite conventionally the son of
a king of the Achaemenid clan of the foremost Persian tribe,
the Pasargadae, "from which," on one ancient authority,
"spring all the Persian kings."

It is not, however, the origin of Cyrus that matters to this
narrative so much as his future, for there were just sixty years
to go before Marathon when he seized power—sixty years in
which the Persians were to make the old Assyrian empire
appear as the work of bumbling amateurs.

14 The Persian

To the drive and ruthlessness of the Assyrian emperors the Persian rulers brought a certain restraint, a diplomatic edge, a capacity for the popular response, which enabled them to win not only lands but often the hearts of their fellow-men.

Xenophon wrote of Cyrus that "He was able to extend the fear of himself over so great a part of the world that he astonished all." Yet, added the Greek, he was also able "to inspire all with a great desire of pleasing him . . . to be governed by his opinion."

Later, when the Persian poet Firdausi fashioned ancient legend into an epic history of the Heroic Age of his people, he reflected this paradox, the composite of savagery and sensibility which sustained Asia's greatest empire. Firdausi's princes dispense and endure dire extremities. Jamshid, the legendary founder of Persepolis, was bound to two boards and sawn into halves with the backbone of a fish. The great champion Rustum, having tragically slain his own son, Sohrab, perished in a pit prepared for the purpose by his brother. Monsters might demand and receive their daily rations in human brains, as did the terrible Zohak, nevertheless there are passages of respect for life and nature amid all this morbidity which echo the healthier tradition of Zoroaster. "Pain not the ant that drags the grain along the ground; it has life, and life is sweet and pleasant to all who possess it," says Erij, heir to the ancient throne. Admittedly, he was about to be murdered at the time, and his disembodied head embalmed by his kinsmen, but in the fabled plea of Erij lay the historical lesson which distinguished Persian rule from Assyrian—namely, that the simple desire to be left alone to live in their own humble fashion was enough for most people, and that those who granted it might reign with relative impunity.

Cyrus was an astute exponent of the two-handed offer—the friendly palm or the mailed fist. What little remains of him in stone and stylus suggests a robust, clean-shaven man, bluff and dynamic, with a folksy wit. That he enjoyed popularity seems certain. His takeover of Media, once effected, was accepted with such apparent complacency by the Medes themselves that the Greeks never really regarded the state as having fallen. Median life was respected, Medes received high posts under Cyrus, and if Herodotus can be believed, even the deposed king came off pretty lightly: "As for Astyages, Cyrus did him no further harm, and kept him in his own house till Astyages died." Indeed, the Persian usurper had barely settled on his new throne before he was contemplating a campaign which would take him, and the bulk of his forces, further from the capital than any Aryan monarch had yet ventured. It was not the plan of a man distrustful of the mood of his subjects.

From the outset of his imperial adventure, Cyrus was blessed by an apathetic regime in Babylonia. A few years before the coup in Media, Babylon had crowned a prince named Nabonidus. Nabonidus was an odd king. He had nothing of Nebuchadnezzar's martial capacity, nor, it seems, much positive interest of any kind in politics. His consuming passions were religion—the patronizing of the cults and temples of the river lands—and archaeology. Forever pulling down old walls to discover the names inscribed on their foundation stones, Nabonidus passed his time carefully compiling lists of the old dynasts—an occupation of unquestionable value to scholarship but of limited value to government.

While Nabonidus reigned, introversive and preoccupied, Cyrus could reasonably turn from his immediate neighbor to concentrate on affairs in the far west. There the death of Alyattes of Lydia had led to a tussle for succession in which the heir apparent had been bested by his half-brother, Croesus. As a result, the family ties contrived by Cyaxares and Alyattes after the battle of the eclipse had become a worthless insurance against further conflict.

Indeed, the reputation of Croesus was distinctly provocative. The extraordinary wealth which allowed him to dominate Asia Minor by buying or compelling the cooperation of the Greek colonists, and generally consolidating and even widening the bounds set by Alyattes, became a byword in east and west.

The Greeks acknowledged his fame in many stories, the best being a mordant little parable—it ought to be true, but unfortunately is not—about a meeting between Croesus and the Athenian lawgiver Solon. Croesus, in the lines of this invention, shows Solon his immense wealth, then asks the Greek who is the happiest man he has ever met—confident, of course, of the answer. To the king's amazement, the sage cites a trio of untitled Greeks who died poor in the service of the gods and their fellows. Croesus dismisses him as an idiot. The irony of the tale for the Greeks who fostered it lay in their hindsight of the clash between Croesus and Cyrus, and what was to come of it.

Hostility—while implicit in the nature of the two kings, both of whom flaunted aggressive confidence—became determinate when Lydia initiated an alliance with Egypt and Babylon. At the same time, Croesus pursued a judiciously philhellenic policy, heaping rich gifts on Delphi and flirting with other Greek shrines. According to tradition, he consulted the Delphic oracle on the wisdom of challenging the Persian interest in Cappadocia. The response, it seems, was in character. If Croesus attacked the Persians, the priests reported, he would destroy a great power. Undeterred by the ambiguity, the king dispatched ambassadors to Sparta loaded with inducements to an armed alliance, allocated gold for Asian mercenaries, and in the spring of 546 B.C., left Sardis and marched east for the Halys.

Simultaneously, Cyrus was heading west. In fact, just who had anticipated whom is a moot point. One thing, however, is

clear enough: Cyrus had no intention of standing by and letting Lydia, Egypt and Bablylonia gang up on him.

By winter's end, Cyrus's own army was prepared for the big
haul to the Halys. The route was a problem. It was a thousand
miles or more from Ecbatana to Lydia, and the mountainous
northern passage through Armenia was still snowbound. The
Persian could not afford to be held up. He wanted Croesus
before his allies could join him. Cyrus decided on the bold
course of marching directly across the plains north of Babylon
to the upper waters of the Euphrates, thence into the Taurus
Mountains. It meant exposing his flank to Nabonidus, but as
Cyrus doubtless surmised, the chances of that monarch rousing
himself from his academic interests were not great.

The march succeeded brilliantly. Sweeping over the lowlands, then into the tangled hills screening Asia Minor, the
toiling Aryan column—tough-soled footmen, rugged horsemen, laden camel trains—passed the sites of modern Sivas and
Tokat and struck purposefully through Cappadocia.

The two armies drew together near Pteria, a city now lost
in the dust of time. Cyrus extended the open hand. After weeks
of exertion and danger on the turbulent trails of a still im-
mensely hazardous continent, he rested his army while his
messengers parleyed. The two rulers could be friends, he said.
Croesus could keep his lands, his palaces and his treasures; all
that was required of him was that he should exchange his
crown for the viceregal emblem of Persia, accepting Cyrus as
his overlord. The alternative was the mailed fist. Psychologi-
cally, the technique was an advance on the tactics of the old
Iranian war lords, who fought first and talked, if at all, afterward. By presenting a choice, albeit a loaded one, it gave Cyrus
the spurious dignity of fake statesmanship, and left room for
doubt, however slight, on the other side.

Croesus rejected the Persian terms loftily. But by late summer the conclusion that he might well have done better to sink
his pride was a tempting one.

After a fairly even opening, the Cappadocian campaign

swung in favor of the tenacious and numerically superior Aryans, forcing Croesus to retire in some disarray to Sardis. Any hope in his mind that the approach of winter and an overextended line of enemy communications might constrain Cyrus proved a delusion. Traditionally nomadic, accustomed to enduring harsh elements, the eastern army pressed forward inexorably.

Croesus had no choice but to fight again. He stood in the valley of the Hermus, otherwise known as the Gediz, before his golden capital, with the famed Lydian cavalry forming his main strength. And here Cyrus employed the ruse which, had he done nothing else in his life, would have endeared him to generations of small boys. At the suggestion, it is said, of his Median general, Harpagus, the Persian king covered his advance with camels from the baggage train. As the ungainly, evil-smelling beasts lumbered forward, the frightened horses of Croesus became unmanageable, the battle became a rout, and the surviving Lydians took refuge with their monarch in Sardis.

The end was not long delayed. From Assyria the Persians and Medes had learned the finer skills of siege warfare. Within a couple of weeks, the city had fallen—the world's richest throne toppled by a people yet counted among civilization's poorest folk.

Thus, the year 546 had closed on a momentous note: Croesus exiled to Media, Cyrus triumphant. If the Persian, in his first bid as emperor had knocked out not only the most resourceful power in Asia but also the least accessible to his capital, who could oppose him without fear? It was not a question many cared to ponder. For the Greeks the collapse of Croesus seemed a cataclysmic event beyond mortal ingenuity: some form of divine retribution for his rather disgusting wealth —perhaps levied by Nemesis, a goddess noted for her moral indignation.

There is a deeply pervasive feeling among the human race

that excessive good fortune will be followed by an accounting of ill-fate, a sort of heavenly invoice. By such reckoning, Croesus had been a doomed man. The story of his encounter with Solon spelled the moral. As Herodotus put it: "To many a man god gives happiness for a while, then casts him down in utter ruin." Envy no one before his death.

If abstract justice was credible, Cyrus, an obscure figure from a remote land, scarcely ranked as a convincing explanation for anything. Not even the Asiatic Greeks had taken him seriously. Both the Ionians and their northern kinsmen the Aeolians had ignored his invitation to side with him against Croesus. More perversely, they had also declined to join the Lydians.

Now with the Persians victorious on their doorstep, the colonists had cause to regret their insularity. Hastening to the conqueror, they asked him to ratify the accommodation they had reached with Croesus. It was said that Cyrus laughed and replied with a fable: "A piper saw some fishes in the sea and played his pipe, hoping they would come and dance with him on land. They would not. So he took a net, caught the fishes and dragged them ashore. And when he saw them leaping in the net he told them to stop dancing, since they had not wished to dance when he had played to them."

Cyrus knew as little of the Greeks as they of him, but with the rest of Asia Minor in his pocket he had no intention of leaving at its furthermost extremity a batch of puny settlements to their own devices. He demanded unconditional surrender.

For the first time the Ionians and their Aeolian neighbors pulled their heads from the sand and tried to act in concert. Unfortunately, the tradition of Greek politics, circumscribed by the independent nature of the city-state, was against them, and Cyrus made the most of it. When Miletus, the strongest of the Ionian cities, was offered and accepted special terms, the alliance was a lost cause. With no great originality, the rest of the settlements sought aid from Sparta. The same step had not saved Croesus, and though this time the Spartans actually turned up, it was hardly in daunting strength. Indeed, a single boat of fifty oars made the journey bearing an official named Lacrines. His orders appear to have been to find out just who this Cyrus was, and to give him a bit of a lecture against worrying the Asian Greeks.

The Persian's response was a dry one. He knew little, he said, of the Spartans, but he understood that they, like other Greeks, had a place set aside in their city "where they gather together to forswear themselves and cheat one another." Well, they had best beware or they "shall not have the misfortunes of the Ionians to talk about, but their own troubles." So saying, he contemptuously departed to Ecbatana, leaving his lieutenants to deal with the Greek colonies. They did so effectively. Herodotus, in a brief account of what followed, says that the citizens manned their fortifications and simply waited to be attacked. All thought of federation came to nothing. However heroic, defense in isolation had no chance. "They were defeated, and on their surrender remained where they were and obeyed the laws laid upon them."

It was not entirely so. So bitterly did some resent the loss of their autonomy, the lapse into "servitude," that they chose exile. The inhabitants of two little cities, Teos and Phocaea, flung their goods on shipboard and sailed away under the noses of the conquerors, the former to lay fresh foundations in Thrace, the latter as far as Marseilles in the western Mediterranean, and Tarshish on the Atlantic coast of Iberia.

Those who remained "obeyed the laws" but cherished their ideals in suppression. Beyond the comprehension of the feudalistic Cyrus, the Greek ideal of political liberty nevertheless clung to the fingers of his empire. Persia had not heard the last of the Ionians.

Hungry Giant

While Nabonidus of Babylon supervised his temple excavations, made offerings to the gods and hobnobbed with the priesthood, his son Belshazzar took a hand in affairs of state. He was, it seems, about as effective as his father. Little is known of the politics of the ancient kingdom at this time, but it would have been surprising had not informed people there felt increasingly uneasy at the boldness of Persia and the apparent indifference of their own leaders.

The supposed alliance with Lydia had proved a non-starter. When Cyrus marched west for Asia Minor across the river lands, blatantly contemptuous of Bablyonia, Nabonidus did nothing. When Persia, with the bulk of its forces a thousand miles removed, was wide open to intervention, Belshazzar was content to sit at home with his army. When Croesus fell and the threat of Cyrus loomed unmistakably over Babylon, what steps did its monarch take to secure his kingdom? On the evidence, precious few. Nothing is heard of his activities to protect its fruitful lands, its flourishing commerce and the busy cities of its dominions from a covetous and voracious neighbor. Instead, the reports make much of his concern for the artifacts of the temples, especially the images of the gods of Ur, Uruk and elsewhere, which he uprooted and carried within the walls of Babylon. Neither priests nor worshipers appreciated his solicitude. Confusion and resentment grew.

In some quarters the prospect of a Persian invasion was even welcomed. Babylonia contained many people enslaved and imported by the predecessors of Nabonidus. The Jews of Israel, taken by Nebuchadnezzar, were such a people. They bitterly resented their captors and their squad of strange gods. Moreover, the striking affinity between Judaism and the Persian beliefs evolved from Zoroaster signaled hope to them from the east. That they regarded Cyrus as a seemly instrument for their release from the bonds of Babylon is suggested in the words of Isaiah:

> Thus saith the Lord to his anointed, to Cyrus, whose right hand I have holden, to subdue nations before him, and I will loose the loins of kings; to open the doors before him, and the gates shall not be shut; I will go before thee. . . . I will break in pieces the doors of brass, and cut in sunder the bars of iron
> . . .

Cyrus, who showed a gracious disposition to acknowledge any god who might serve his purposes, embarked on the reduction of Babylonia in 538 B.C. In normal circumstances it should have proved a formidable undertaking. No throne in the world was surrounded by such awesome bastions as that of Babylon, its inner citadel protected by triple ramparts, its ramparts screened by extensive dikes and extra walls, the whole flanked by two great rivers.

But without the will of the people to resist, the machinery of defense is futile, and the Babylonians, poorly led and discordant, had no heart for the contest. Cyrus fell on Belshazzar's army at Opis, north of Babylon, and routed it at a single stroke. At the same time, a Persian general named Gobryas marched directly on the capital, which he entered "without skirmish or battle." Belshazzar was slain; Nabonidus surrendered.

Cyrus, astutely conscious of the advantages of posing as a deliverer rather than a conqueror, ordered that city and populace were to be respected. To the natives of Babylon he offered himself as the servant of their foremost god, Marduk. "The great lord Marduk," proclaimed Cyrus solemnly, "looked joyously on the caring for his people. To his city he sent me as friend and companion. Numerous as the waters of a river, my troops marched with him. Without battle or conflict, he permitted me to enter Babylon. He spared this city of Babylon a calamity." If the protection of his victims was a shrewd move, the relinquishing of credit to their own god was a shrewder one. When Cyrus not only gave public worship to Marduk but returned the provincial gods to their cities, the new regime was assured of a smooth start.

From Marduk the Persian turned grandly to the Jewish god. As emperor of Babylon, Cyrus became overlord of Judah. He marked his prerogative by commanding that the temple of Jehovah in Jerusalem, destroyed by Nebuchadnezzar, be rebuilt at the expense of the empire, and that any Babylonian Jews who wished to return home should be free to do so. The gesture was not entirely magnanimous. Those Jews most useful to Babylon had established their talents comfortably and had no desire for repatriation among the hostile tribes of Palestine. On the other hand, those who did want resettlement acquired usefulness thereby, for, dependent upon the protection of Cyrus, they formed a loyal outpost in the southwest—most conveniently covering the gateway to Egypt.

With Babylon now the second capital of the empire, after Ecbatana, Cyrus appointed his son Cambyses to govern it while turning his own attention to broader fields. Restlessly he roamed Asia campaigning, expanding his dominions. His triumphs in the east are hazier than those to the west, but it is known that he skirted the vast wastelands of the Iranian plateau to conquer Bactria, subdue the best part of what is now Afghanistan and push north across the Oxus to the Jaxartes, where he left his name in the town of Cyropolis (Kodjend). Indeed, from 546 to his death in 529 B.C., Cyrus was indefatigable, marching and countermarching, fighting and conquering, remorselessly bludgeoning and inveigling people into submission.

Many were his hard-driven warriors buried in distant parts. There is a legend that he lost an entire army in the wilds of

Baluchistan, a land duly added to the empire, but more often than not the dusty, weathered columns returned to Ecbatana victorious, their baggage trains loaded with exotic tributes. It is three thousand miles from the blue Aegean to the muddy Jaxartes, and that as the crow flies. Before he had finished, Cyrus could ride from one to the other and be welcomed at every stage by his vassals or governors. In less than two decades, this remarkable adventurer had dominated more of the earth than any king before him had dared contemplate, let alone negotiate.

His last days are wrapped in mystery. According to the Greeks, Cyrus the Great was killed on the wild steppe east of the Caspian, fighting a people beyond the Jaxartes, the Massagetai. Herodotus says that the Persian demanded their queen in marriage, and when refused, invaded the country. Following the fatal battle, his story goes, the queen plunged the lifeless head of Cyrus in a pool of gore, exclaiming, "I give thee thy fill of blood." This seems rather unlikely for it is known that the Persians retired bearing the corpse of their fallen king to Pasargadae, the homeland of his tribal ancestors, where it was laid in a simple and stately tomb (it still stands, though long since desecrated by graverobbers) on a terraced plinth of huge stones.

"I am Cyrus, King of Kings," ran his cryptic epitaph. To the people of his day, it said enough.

The Persian empire passed lawfully to the conqueror s oldest son, Cambyses (or Kambuzia), a man of maturity on his father's death. He had already governed Babylon, but rule over the greatest realm in the world was another thing.

Two preliminaries were needed to set him off on the right foot. One was to secure his succession against rivals; the other, to ensure the continuity of the line in the advent of his own death. Both were family matters. The main challenge to his rule was his younger brother, Smerdis, or Bardiya, who enjoyed too much popularity, it seems, for the comfort of Cambyses, a severe and not greatly beloved man. Cambyses is said to have flayed one of his judges for corruption and had the man's skin stretched over his judicial chair. For a king of such reputation, the problem of a troublesome brother was not a big one. Smerdis quietly disappeared. The ugly deed was in the royal tradition of assassination, but in this case it was hushed up. Meanwhile the second consideration, that of producing an heir whose ties were wholly with the family, was regulated by another trusted tradition. Persian kings, as indeed others before them, frequently married their sisters in the search for pure issue. Cambyses wed two of his, Atossa and Roxana.

Domestic matters thus settled, he was ready to tackle affairs of a grander kind. From Cyrus the new king had inherited one major item of outstanding business. Unlike the great princes of Nineveh, the Persian conqueror had not lived to claim the homage of Egypt, where an aged ruler named Amasis now occupied the throne of Memphis.

Cambyses prepared to put the matter right. Drawing from the seagoing people of his empire, the Ionian Greeks and the Phoenicians of the Levant, he organized a navy to sail on the Nile delta. Then, mustering the veteran army trained by Cyrus, he marched to Gaza, the last township of importance before the bleak desert strip separating Palestine from the subcontinent of Africa.

His reported entourage was versatile. Among his comforts was his younger wife, Roxana. Among his counselors was the elderly and deposed Croesus, now apparently a sage in the Persian camp. And among his senior lieutenants was a certain Darius, a shrewd captain and the scion of a family of royal blood.

The Egyptian position was unenviable. It was less than a century since the army of the Nile had been bested by Nebuchadnezzar. Since then, the power of Egypt had not progressed, yet Persia had grown like a hungry giant. Amasis enjoyed prestige at home as a statesman and strategist, but he was an old man and events abroad had gone against him. He had seen first Croesus and then Nabonidus overwhelmed. He had worked at a friendship with the Greeks through Delphi, contributing handsomely to the rebuilding of its temple, but the governments of mainland Greece were not galvanized by affairs across five hundred miles of water, and the Asian Greeks were under Persian domination. He had cultivated a particularly close relationship with Samos, a Greek island off the coast of Ionia. When Samos, convinced of the invincibility of the Persians, not only declined to aid Amasis but actually placed ships at the disposal of Cambyses, the future looked black indeed for Egypt.

There was still, however, one ally to be counted, and that impervious to human fickleness: between Gaza and Egypt lay the desert—a relatively short stretch as some deserts go, but an unyielding one, whose hot, featureless sands, blinding dust storms and total aridity had doomed many an earlier traveler. For Cambyses and his army it meant a punishing march of perhaps ten days, unsheltered from sun and parching wind, with the prospect of facing a fresh and impassioned resistance at the end of it.

Luck was with the Persians. At the last moment, a mercenary officer in the employ of Amasis deserted and brought a body of desert nomads into the invading camp. With their help, a relay of camel trains was set up to shuttle water to Cambyses as his troops advanced. If this was not enough to dismay the Egyptians, Amasis was taken ill on the eve of the Persian assault and died suddenly, leaving his fearful nation in the hands of an untried son.

Psammeticus, the new king, commenced his defense with the right move, challenging the Persians as they emerged from the desert at Pelusium, east of the sustaining delta country. Both sides fought desperately.

The outcome was critical. The Egyptians struggled for their

homes and sovereignty; the invaders fought in the knowledge that a retreat into the desert they had just crossed could be disastrous. (Eighty years later, according to Herodotus, the battlefield was still strewn with skulls and bleached bones.) But the Egyptians could not hold back the aggressive Aryans, and at the day's end, a shaken Psammeticus made his second and fatal move. Instead of retiring to the defensible waterways of the delta, where he might have regrouped his army and found room to maneuver, he retreated to Memphis and shut himself within the city.

As a military expedient, taking refuge in a stronghold makes sense when relief may be forthcoming, or when the enemy is unprepared to prolong his engagement. Otherwise, it is simply inviting checkmate. Psammeticus had no hope of relief and no hope that the Persians, with the resources of the land for the taking, would go away. At Sardis, and against the Ionian cities, they had demonstrated their adeptness at siege warfare. Now, though Memphis resisted stubbornly, they tightened their stranglehold and waited. The end was inevitable.

The fall of the city in 525 B.C. was the fall of Egypt.

In some ways, the conquest was more dramatic even than that of Babylon or Lydia, for the brilliance of Egyptian history surpassed the dreams of any Persian, and the splendor of its symbols must have filled the rude warriors of Cambyses with wonder and a powerful euphoria. To have conquered Egypt was to have mastered the last of the great independent kingdoms of the ancient world.

16 Darius Disposes

Events, like the winged god Mazda of imperial Persia, were flying. The sixth century B.C. was in its final quarter and the generation that would provide the warriors for Marathon was now born. Within four years of Cambyses's Egyptian triumph the legal successor to Cyrus would perish and the spiritual successor rise from the ranks of his young officers. The tale is a bizarre one, and begins with that madness which attacks many conquerors.

Conquest is an addictive habit. Cambyses, having picked it up from his father, was now driven to satisfy a mounting lust. From the pinnacle of Memphis, the invitation seemed to lie at his very feet: having occupied the land of the Pharaohs, he would conquer all Africa.

His notion of Africa, however, was a bit vague. To the south, the Africa of the ancients ended in Ethiopia. Here the gods held their nocturnal revels—or, at least, so thought Homer, who had an idea that the sun spent the night there. The Ethiopians, or "dark-faced" people, were known as resourceful, organized and good soldiers, for in the eighth century they had actually dominated Egypt. As Cambyses understood the route, reaching Ethiopia from Egypt meant crossing Nubia, a barren land, old in culture, whose black inhabitants (and those who still think the black race has no history may take note) had been manufacturing distinctively decorated pottery and ingeniously barbed spears thousands of years before the rise of Persia. To the west of the Nile delta, the Persians were aware of Carthage, in the region of modern Tunis, a maritime city frequented by Greeks, Phoenicians and others. Around the coasts of the empire, Carthage was highly regarded as a trading port. Between

Egypt and Carthage lay the Libyan desert. Cambyses, now a trifle blasé about deserts, believed the problem could be overcome by hopping from oasis to oasis. It must be added, however, that he did not attempt it personally. Instead, the emperor reserved himself for the bid on Ethiopia, dispatching a separate force from his army in Egypt into Libya. The army never reached Carthage, nor did it come back. According to Egyptian tradition, the expedition simply disappeared in the wilderness, which is not inconceivable, since there is enough desert west of the delta to make the strip east to Gaza look very insignificant.

The southern campaign was just as futile. Cambyses, moving on Ethiopia by land and river, got no further than Nubia. If the king of that country can be believed, the Nubians destroyed the Persian fleet. The land forces, prostrated by the broiling wastes, managed to limp back to Egypt.

So much for the conquest of Africa!

The failure had a profound effect on Cambyses. Initially, following the example of Cyrus, he had gone to some lengths to accommodate sentiments in Egypt—adopting the costume, customs and religion of the Pharaohs. But now stories spread of unstable, near-maniacal behavior. It was said that he slew the sacred Apis bull of Egypt in a fit of temper, ridiculed and burned the statues of Egyptian gods, opened ancient sepulchers and ogled the mummies. There were rumors of dark deeds in his own camp. He was supposed to have murdered his wife Roxana by a kick in the abdomen, and having ordered the slaying of Croesus on some pretext, countermanded the order and vent his spleen on the frustrated assassins.

Darius, who was close to Cambyses in Egypt, later scorned the spate of lurid gossip from the Nile lands. "Untruth," he averred, "had spread all over the country, not only in Persia and Media, but in other provinces." And, indeed, it was wise to be skeptical of scandal surrounding the private lives of powerful men, not because their behavior is exemplary—far from it—

but because they command the wherewithal to keep their scandals quiet.

Nevertheless, there seems no doubt that the emperor was depressed when he left Egypt for home in the spring of 521 B.C. On top of his African disasters, news was coming through of rebellion in Persia. Having settled the governorship of his Nile dominion, he followed the circuitous homeward trail through Gaza and Damascus, taking Darius with him.

Somewhere in Syria, perhaps Damascus or Hamath, Cambyses, son of Cyrus, passed out of history. Darius records the moment in an enigmatic line: "He died his own death." This has been construed as a verdict of suicide, a plausible theory in the face of continuing setbacks. Yet it could also mean that the king died of an accidentally self-inflicted injury, which fits with Greek tradition. Herodotus thought he came to grief mounting his charger.

At all events, leadership of the returning Africa veterans now devolved on Darius. By good fortune, a marvelous introduction to Darius has survived in a huge inscription he had carved on rock at Behistun, on the road to Ecbatana. Not only does it give his own version of the continuing tale of Persian destiny, it provides a portrait of the man himself, for amid the text is a splendid sculpture of the despot, thick-bearded, straight-backed, with a rich mustache and a long, slightly curved nose. There seems no reason to doubt the Behistun inscription, though its theme is a prodigious one.

Early in his reign, it will be remembered, Cambyses had contrived the secret murder of his popular brother, Smerdis. When the Egyptian expedition was launched, Persia had been left in the hands of a certain Oropastes, one of the few people, it appears, with knowledge of the assassination. Now, by a curious coincidence, Oropastes had a brother, Gaumata, who bore some resemblance to the dead Smerdis. Between them, they hit on an audacious scheme by which Gaumata would claim the throne in the guise of the murdered man. With the developing remoteness and seclusion of the oriental palace, this was less improbable than it might seem. That the mass of ordinary people could distinguish one member of the royal family from another is unlikely, and the conspirators had no qualms about silencing the few who could.

The pseudo-Smerdis arose to wide acclaim, smoothing his path with wholesale exemptions from taxation and war service. News of the death of Cambyses reached him as a gratuitous bonus. For a moment it looked as though one of the most brazen frauds in ancient history had paid off.

But Gaumata had reckoned without Darius. On his return to Persia, Darius found the false Smerdis enthroned and the tribal chiefs, though in many cases skeptical and indignant, overawed by the usurper's popular following. Darius was neither fooled nor acquiescent. Behind him, the dusty column of hardened campaigners, travel-weary but loyal to their leader, provided the means of opposition. Gathering half a dozen chiefs about him, Darius burst into the castle where Gaumata was staying and slew him before he had time to call his guards out. A swift massacre of the impostor's supporters was organized in Ecbatana, where his severed head was revealed to the populace. The crown it had briefly worn was donned by Darius.

The position of the new king was perilous. He had gained the palace, but general recognition was a different thing. The pedigree claimed by Darius was a lofty one, sharing ancestry with Cyrus, but it lacked the force of direct descent from the emperors. He hastened to shore it up. Already wed to a daughter of Gobryas, the general who had first seized Babylon for Persia, Darius now took as wife, among others, two widows of Cambyses, including the ill-fated Roxana's sister, Atossa, and a daughter of the legitimate Smerdis, one Parmys. Of at least six of his senior wives, two were daughters of Cyrus. In Persia his standing became more assured.

But his hold on the empire was tenuous. Neither Cyrus nor

Cambyses had consolidated their conquests through any form of central administration. Governors had been appointed, then left largely to their own devices. They had their own troops and even, in some cases, their own fleets. Only their loyalty to, or fear of, Persia, held the empire together. The temptation to exploit their virtual autonomy was considerable, and in the confusion which followed the death of Cambyses, it became overwhelming.

The storm of revolution broke in that incorrigible trouble spot of olden days, Elam. Cyrus had resurrected Susa as an important center of the empire, and here a leader named Atrina, or Ashina, proclaimed independence.

Almost immediately rebellion followed elsewhere. In Babylon, Media, Armenia and even Persia itself, pretenders, declaring links with the old kings, mustered sizable armies. To the east, the plateau land of Sargartia and the northerly highlands of Margiana rang with the cries of insurrection.

His order challenged on all sides, Darius responded viciously. Reconquest, or counterinsurrection, exposes the latent brutality in regimes based on coercion. As a general rule, men defend their proprietorial interests more savagely than they establish them. Thus Cyrus, winning new lands, had often been lenient with his opponents; Darius, fighting to hold those gains, was not. Thralldom could be reimposed, his acts suggest, only by mortal fear.

Overall, Darius was far from barbaric. Indeed, the totality of his reign suggests an emperor of much greater sophistication than Cyrus. Yet now, with all that had been grasped turning sour on him, he matched vigor with a barbarity unrevealed in the great conqueror.

Atrina of Susa fell quickly. Betrayed by his countrymen, he was surrendered to Darius, who slew him with his own hand. In Media, the rebel Phraortes was a tougher proposition. His influence spread into Armenia, and four battles were needed to crush it, the last resulting in the flight and capture of the local leader. Phraortes was carried to Ecbatana, where Darius, to use his own unabashed words, "cut off his nose, and his ears, and his tongue and put out his eyes," then displayed him in fetters as a grisly warning of imperial wrath before impaling him. The wretched prisoner could hardly have suffered more sickeningly had the most savage of Assyrian monarchs got hold of him. The next victim was the instigator of the uprising in Sargartia. Before being crucified he was mutilated in the same merciless fashion as Phraortes. Among others, a Persian dissident named Vahyazdata met an equally horrific end.

Militarily, the manner in which Darius deployed his limited forces and his few trusty generals was masterly. Within three years of his accession he had crushed eight rebellions, at one stage fighting on three fronts at the same time.

Perhaps his outstanding campaign was against the Babylonians, who rose in strength behind a leader who claimed descent from Nebuchadnezzar. Darius, taking the field in person, was stopped at the Tigris by a large force established on the far bank. After an astute diversionary maneuver involving camel troops, he gained a crossing, got the best of two engagements and finally trapped the rebels in Babylon. For almost two years, Darius sustained the siege of the city, simultaneously coordinating operations elsewhere. The capture of Babylon in 519 marked the turn of the crisis. By the year's end, the authority of the new emperor was in little doubt. To be quite sure, he purged the dominions of suspects. In Lydia, the governor was put to death by his own guards on secret orders from Darius, who, revisiting Egypt, summarily executed the governor there, too. At the same time, an administrative system was introduced to prevent a recrudescence of provincial ambitions. In place of the old-style governor, three officers were appointed to each land: a satrap (or viceroy), a general and a secretary of state. These posts were mutually independent and individually responsible to the emperor. As a double safeguard, this divide-and-rule policy was backed by a body of touring inspectors with authority to investigate and punish abuses. The system was a great success.

With the empire pacified, Darius showed his true genius. Brilliant as he had proved at war and hideous in retribution, it was as a constructive ruler—an organizer, builder, lawgiver and statesman—that he really excelled. His progress was methodical. The satrapies were assessed for tribute on a rational basis—poor lands such as Baluchistan owing the lowest revenues, rich lands such as Egypt owing most, the taxes payable in kind as well as money. He was the first Persian monarch to produce coinage, and the daric (not, in fact, named after Darius but from a local word meaning gold) became international currency. His interest in promoting the commerce of the empire led to exploration. He mounted a maritime expedition under an Asian Greek named Scylax, who explored the coast from the mouth of the Indus to Suez, and he had a canal dug from Suez to the Nile to enable his ships to sail from Egypt to Persia via the Red Sea. His commercial fleets made connections with Carthage, Sicily and Italy.

Darius proclaimed the "true religion" of Zoroaster earnestly. The great sculpture at Behistun incorporated the winged symbol of Mazda, as did the royal seal. Gold and silver tablets, prepared with inscriptions in three languages, acknowledged the debt he owed his deity: "Darius the great king, king of kings, king of the lands, says: This realm I hold, from Scythia which is beyond Sogdiana to Ethiopia, from India to Sardis, was granted me by Ahura Mazda, the greatest god. May Ahura Mazda protect me and my household."

Nevertheless, the emperor encouraged the Jews and Egyptians to build temples to their own gods, and bestowed favors on the oracles of the Ionians. Like Cyrus, he recognized the influence of the priesthood, irrespective of race or creed, and used it resolutely to further his diplomacy. After his bitter debut he was widely successful in establishing good will in the empire.

Where good will failed, notably on its wilder fringes, Darius employed the great imperial and colonial armies he had organized. Never before had the despotic combination of threat and benevolence been exercised on such a scale or so efficiently.

By the turn of the century, two decades from his accession, Darius had taken an edifice on the verge of a collapse as dramatic as that of the Assyrian empire and fashioned from it a monster of obedience ranging, as he himself said, from India to the Aegean, from the burning sands of Africa to the frozen peaks abutting China.

Persian power stood at its zenith. The idea that such power might be defied by a few thousand Greek citizens can only have seemed to the court at Ecbatana quite preposterous.

Part 3
In Which the Despot Snarls

By divine decree destiny was potent of old, and enjoined on Persians to engage in wars, and cavalry routs, and the overthrow of cities.

—Aeschylus, *The Persae*

Cyrus had been hugely amused, we are told, to learn that the citizens of Greece congregated in public places to govern themselves by what he derisively pictured as vulgar argument and popular ignorance. Even today, when government by the people has long lost its novelty, there is no shortage of men, or women for that matter, who find democratic processes contemptible.

Motives apart, those who seek power are not looking for debate but for obedience. For a general, in particular, obedience is imperative, and it could only have seemed extraordinary to Cyrus that ordinary people, the rank and file, should be involved in decisions of state, whether vital or trivial.

In Athens a minor fiscal resolution, or the impeachment of a single citizen, demanded a quorum of thousands and a possible orgy of oratory. The emperor of Persia might decide to double the taxes of a country, or punish an entire populace, in the flash of a moment—and heaven help anyone who questioned him. Across most of the ancient world, there was no doubting which system worked. Autocracy was traditional; democracy, revolutionary.

Darius had dressed the despotic office with a few liberal frills, but relinquished none of the authority. As a reward for supporting his accession, an elite group of noble families enjoyed consultative privileges and, in council, could address the king freely. But *consultative* was the key word. Final decisions were the emperor's.

Democracy, to the extent he understood it, must have seemed rather infantile, or at least a feeble threat, for eventually the Asiatic Greeks of the empire were allowed to indulge their strange whim, though at a strictly municipal level. To the Persians, it was a droll charade. The citizens of Ionia could talk all they liked; in the end, they did what the satrap of the province decreed, and the satrap took his orders from Darius.

That there was a good deal to laugh at in Greek politics did not elude the Greeks. In Athens, on assembly days, public slaves drove tardy citizens toward the Pnyx with a rope smothered in ruddle, or red chalk. Anyone later found with red on his clothing might be fined for neglecting his civic responsibility.

Aristophanes poked fun at the foibles of the assembly in the *Acharnians*, a comedy about an old countryman who is so fed up with the Peloponnesian War that he makes a private treaty with Sparta. At the beginning of the play, the old man arrives punctually at the Pnyx hoping to discuss peace, only to find that nobody has turned up. "They are all talking in the market and running away from the ruddled rope." At last, the members of the presiding committee appear, jostling for the best seats, the benches fill and the meeting proceeds to business—ignoring all need for peace talks. So furious becomes the honest rustic that he declares he can feel a drop of rain, a pronouncement sufficient to send everyone bustling home. Aristophanes is very funny and perceptive in his satire, but it is significant that the ability of a society to laugh openly at its ruling institutions is a civilized one, and does not flourish under all regimes.

The really remarkable thing about the Athenian assembly was not that some citizens were less than punctilious in attendance, nor that a thunderstorm or an ill omen might disrupt proceedings, but that the great majority of eligible Athenians did attend, and that such debates as can be glimpsed in the records appear to have been long, lively and basically orderly.

Democratic Athenians believed in the sovereignty of the popular will, yet recognized the chaos which would accrue unless this was arrived at through formal procedures. For a start, all new business had to go through the council. The council then proposed a line of action for acceptance, amendment or rejection by its fellow citizens. If a debate was called for, speakers were invited by a herald. While everyone had a right to be heard, debate tended fairly naturally to be dominated by certain individuals of flair, the so-called "orators" or "comers forward." The audience had its favorites, and was neither patient nor polite with incompetent performers. Finally, the assembly normally voted by a show of hands, its decision then becoming binding. It should be added, however, that its business was limited to current policies and did not intrude on standing laws, which could be changed or introduced only by a judicial committee of the people after detailed deliberation. The Athenians were not so imprudent as to lay the basic and tested laws of society open to being stood on their heads at every meeting by the emotions of the moment.

Two manifestations of modern democracy were absent from the ancient assembly. Membership was not restricted to chosen representatives of the citizenship: it was the citizenship in total—thus a system based on referendum rather than mandate. And there were no political parties in the formal sense, though, of course, political groups existed as informal expressions of sentiment. As has been seen, there were reactionaries, mostly associated with wealth and bygone privilege, who, at the extreme, hankered for the overthrow of the system itself in favor of oligarchy or tyranny, against which ranged the moderating middle class and the majority of poorer democrats.

On the eve of Marathon it was the orators of the last two groups, the popular champions, who "commanded the stone" (occupied the speakers' platform) in Athens.

In *The Persae* of Aeschylus—the only extant historical drama by a Greek writer—Atossa, wife of Darius, asks the chorus of ancients gathered outside the palace at Susa what despot, since it is not her husband, rules the people of Greece. The chorus replies, with solemn emphasis, that the Greeks are the subjects and slaves of none.

The notion of political freedom beguiled Hellas, yet it had

little history and an uncertain future. Despotism was the common denominator of nations, and the familiar canon to which men had adapted and resigned themselves. Democracy was the great imponderable of the ancient world. Many who had firsthand experience were cautious. Popular government and tyranny interchanged with fickle frequency in the Greek orbit, where the range and splendor of despotic government might be deplored but could hardly be gainsaid.

Greece might have the finest writers, scientists and philosophers of the age, but beside the vast organization of the Persian empire its administration seemed parochial. Greece might have planted its little colonies on distant shores, but when it came to foreign affairs and power diplomacy it was the imperialists of Persia who swept the board. The Spartans might regard their troops with professional pride, the Athenians cherish their citizens' army, but for all their intellectual accomplishment they hefted much the same weapons as the wild warriors of the empire, whose numbers defied contemplation. Even the vaunted Greek gods, incomparably personified, lacked the monopolistic thrall in which the less tangible Mazda held Persia.

Reasonably as the democratic thinkers of the age may have decried despotism as a barrier to the growth of mind and spirit, the lumping of all outsiders as "barbarians" showed less than Greek objectivity. Indeed, the slur is often belied in Greek literature.

Herodotus, born on the Aegean coast of Asia Minor and holding the conflict between East and West as the key to all history, linked the strife with an intriguing episode in which a more candid picture of the Persian foe is revealed.

It happened, so the historian asserted, in this fashion. A certain Democedes, a citizen of the Greek colony of Croton, in Italy, won renown as a surgeon, and being a somewhat venal man, proceeded to hawk his talents in high places. After a profitable engagement in Athens, he sold his services expensively to the tyrant of Samos, an island off Ionia, in whose company he was seized by the satrap of Sardis and eventually dispatched to Darius among a batch of common slaves.

Democedes had not been long in the Persian capital when the emperor injured his foot so severely that the Egyptian doctors tending him (the Egyptians had a famous medical school at Sais and were regarded as preeminent in medicine) could do nothing to stop the pain. At his wit's end, Darius sent for the Greek, who had impressed his skills on the captive community. Democedes, having duly mended the royal foot, was rewarded with gold, given an honored post in the palace, and being a humane man, allowed to plead successfully for the lives of the Egyptian surgeons who had failed to cure the emperor.

Democedes now possessed pretty well everything an ambitious fellow might covet, with one exception: his liberty. And there was even a way of gaining that, for one day the queenly Atossa came to him for a private consultation—and women, as Herodotus was never slow to point out, were quite capable of taking a hand in ancient history. Atossa, it appears, had some form of tumor on her breast. The price Democedes demanded for a cure was that she should engineer his escape from Persia. She agreed, and kept the bargain. Why, she whispered, when next she lay with her husband, did the great king not add Hellas to his empire? Dearly would she like Spartan and Athenian maids to wait on her. At least, he might send Democedes to spy out the land for him. Agreeably, Darius sent for the surgeon, briefed him for the mission and invited him to take a shipload of treasures home to his family before returning to Persia with the intelligence.

Herodotus asserted his own belief that the emperor was sincere in his generosity, but Democedes, fearing a trap, subtly replied that he would rather leave the valuables behind to enjoy when he came back. It seems the king was not entirely trustful, for he assigned an escort of fifteen Persian agents to accompany Democedes and thwart any possible escape bid.

The party embarked at the Phoenician port of Sidon, made

a thorough survey of the coast of Greece, then continued to Greek Tarentum, in Italy. Here the surgeon persuaded the Tarentines to hold his Persian companions as spies while he headed for his native city, Croton. Only when he sent word that he was safely home did the Tarentines release his escort.

With dutiful persistence, the small body of Persians sailed on to Croton, found Democedes in the marketplace, and boldly apprehended him. There followed a sharp encounter with the citizens, who rallied to their fellow countryman despite some argument that he should be given up rather than incur the displeasure of the emperor. In the end, the Persians were packed off.

Democedes was free from Darius, but the story had a pungent sequel. The Persian agents, shipwrecked on their return voyage, were retrieved from their fate and brought safely to Susa by an expatriate Greek named Gillus. Now is was the turn of Gillus to win the gratitude of Darius, and, like Democedes before him, to yearn for restoration to his native city. Unlike Democedes, however, Gillus was not prepared to endanger his compatriots by upsetting the emperor. He remained, instead, in exile.

And so concludes the episode. The contrast between the self-interest of the surgeon and the selflessness of Gillus is clearly stressed. Herodotus has used the anecdote, which need not be accepted too literally, as a parable. His point is that a man chooses between himself and his country, and ought to put his country first. In the Greek mind, freedom meant the freedom of the society rather than of the individual, whose obligations overshadowed his liberties. Herodotus is also concerned with Greek superiority. By implication, the Greeks in his story are cleverer than the Persians, whom Democedes can outwit and Gillus saves from disaster. Naturally, too, they are freedom-loving, altruistic (if not above the need for an occasional lecture on the sin of egoism) and peerless in science, in this case medicine.

But what is really more interesting is the complexion Herodotus places on the Persians, the "barbarians." Darius emerges from the yarn as generous in his gratitude and honorable in his word, as is his wife in keeping her bargain with the doctor. The Persian agents are loyal, brave and resolute. This portrait does not conflict with what is known of the training of the Persian ruling classes. Xenophon and Plato acknowledge the education of the Iranian nobility to have embraced the ideals of wisdom, truthfulness, self-control and fearlessness.

Admittedly, to scratch a Persian noble was to find something pretty primitive: witness the punishments the relatively enlightened Darius inflicted on his enemies. But then, few societies bear much scratching, and the Greeks certainly were not renowned for saintliness.

18   A Bird, a Mouse, a Frog

Whatever thought Atossa may or may not have given to the need for Athenian handmaids, the improbability that the world's greatest ruler conducted the expansion of his empire to obtain domestic servants for his wives hardly needs arguing. In foreign affairs, the strategic considerations of Darius, having once settled the running of his dominions, were strictly practical and straightforward. By the inexorable laws of empire, the Persian colossus had to expand or face contraction.

The emperor's predicament was the classic one. The vast perimeter of his multinational realm was vulnerable. Assuring its defense meant organizing armies; armies, unless occupied to advantage, were costly and often dangerous to keep around; it followed both defensively and economically that the annexation of neighboring territory was preferable to trying to maintain the status quo.

Admitting as much, the choice of regions for conquest was governed primarily by their richness or the threat they posed to the empire. By either of these criteria, the small and isolated city-states of Greece can scarcely have seemed to rate attention. On the other hand, two great areas, each marking a tantalizing extremity of the empire, beckoned irresistibly. To the west, separated from the satrapy of Sardis by the narrow waters of the Hellespont and the Bosphorus, lay the lands of Thrace, leading to Macedonia and northern Greece. To the southwest, the terminal heights of the Iranian plateau looked down on the broad plain of the Punjab.

The Punjab was rich indeed, and though its annexation, and that of Sind, is poorly recorded, it appears that at some time prior to 512 B.C., Darius moved in and established a satrapy

there, the twentieth in his empire. His subsequent revenues
from India were enormous: "a greater tribute than any other
province," wrote Herodotus, who reckoned the annual payment to Persia from this source at 360 talents of gold dust, or
nearly five times the combined contributions of Babylon and
Assyria.

After the Punjab, the emperor turned to Thrace. A few
Greek colonies dotted its Aegean coast, while Darius already
had vassals on the banks of the Hellespont. From these he
would have learned something of the true Thracians. Dark-
complexioned and fond of tattooing, the natives spoke a language closely allied to that of Greece. They were a lusty race.
Their deities included the Greek god of wine, Dionysus; Thracian "goat-men" carried a wooden phallus in their religious
rites; Thracian girls enjoyed complete license before marriage.
More pertinently, Thrace, like the Punjab, promised rich pick-
ings, for gold and silver were worked there. It was also important to the safety of the empire.

Among the marauding races of the ancient world, none was
feared more than the Scythians. The Greeks used the term
rather loosely for the tribes of southern Russia, but left no
doubt of their ferocity. Time and again, these vigorous and
destructive nomads had swept southwest from the steppes of
Kazakh to terrorize the people of Mesopotamia and Asia Minor. Imperial Persia—screened to the east by its outposts on
the double line of the Jaxartes and Oxus, and across its northern aspect by the Caspian, the Caucausus Mountains and the
Black Sea—was relatively well-protected against the swooping
raids of the Scythians. For the most part, its armies could be
deployed with fair warning. But there was a weak spot. In their
westerly prowlings, the Scythians had established themselves
among those other roving despoilers, the Cimmerians, in the
Ukraine, where they did some trading on the Black Sea and
pushed communities around its coast toward the Danube.
Here, only Thrace lay between them and direct access to the

heart of Asia Minor, with its inviting farmlands and the greatest proliferation of urban centers in the empire.

For Darius, the advantages of occupying Thrace were compelling. Apart from blocking the Scythians and providing an added source of revenue, it offered command of the north coast of the Aegean to give him two sides of that profitable trading pool.

In 512 B.C., the emperor embarked on this his first enterprise of aggrandizement in Europe. It was an ambitious one. The Thracians were warlike, he had the Greek settlements to contend with, and there was the possibility of a head-on clash with the Scythians. His expedition needed a powerful bite. Tradition puts its strength at eight hundred thousand men, but statistics were not a strongpoint of ancient historians, and armies have a way of growing with gusto in the recounting of campaign tales. Eighty thousand may well be nearer the actual mark. Even so, it was a huge force for its time. Mobilized from various dominions, this army was brought to the Bosphorus, where Darius, in all his martial splendor, stood at its head.

Plans had been well made. A fleet, commanded by vassal tyrants of the Asiatic Greek ports, had been mustered to support the army on the Thracian coast, and an engineer had been commissioned from the Ionian island of Samos to bridge the strait to Europe. This engineer, Mandrocles, later commemorated his achievement with a picture at the temple of Hera, in Samos. "Having spanned the fishy Bosphorus," ran the gist of its inscription, "Mandrocles dedicated to Hera a memorial of his raft-bridge. A crown he earned for his own head, and glory for the men of Samos, for the job he did pleased King Darius."

Details of the warfare in Thrace are not preserved, but it seems that most of the country prudently submitted without fuss. One tribe, however, is known to have resisted. These people, the Getae, lived in the north, occupying the valley of the Danube, and Darius, having subdued their number on the

Thracian side of the river was faced with their brothers on the far bank. Calling up his fleet, which had entered the Danube from the Black Sea, he ordered that the stream be spanned with the Greek ships. Thus the king crossed, and the ships' crews, left to guard the bridgehead, watched his columns march out of sight.

Darius had credible reasons for traversing the Danube. The Getae to the north had Scythian allies. He needed to instill respect for his new boundary. Moreover, it was reputed that there was gold beyond the river. Doubtless, he wished to see for himself. In Greek history, however, his motives are incredible. According to Herodotus, Darius was not chiefly interested in Thrace but, rather, was consumed with the mad project of conquering Scythia by marching around the Black Sea to the steppes of Russia.

In considering the Greek account of his exploits north of the Danube—and there is none other to go by—it must be remembered that it gained currency at a time when it had become convenient to fault Persian strategies.

The pith of the legend is as follows.

Before crossing the Danube bridge, Darius tied sixty knots in a cord, and handing it to the tyrants commanding the Greek fleet, said to them: "Untie one knot each day, and stay here and guard the bridge until all the knots are untied. If I have not returned in sixty days, you may sail home." Whereupon, he headed north into the great spaces of Scythia.

His uncertainty in estimating a return date was sensible, for fable had plenty of surprises in store for him. Soon the Persians were tramping through a veritable fairyland, a world of travelers' romances in which it was widely believed the gold mines were guarded by griffins and worked by tame ants as large as foxes. Careless of distance, supply problems, the further rivers to negotiate, the emperor supposedly slogged on. Just where he went is not clear, but we see him doggedly marching beyond the Don.

For a long while the natives avoided contact. Then Darius, frustrated, sent a message to the king of the Scythians. "Strange man," observed the emperor, "why do you keep flying before me? If you deem yourself able to resist, cease your wanderings and come, engage in battle. If you are fearful of my strength, even so do not run away. You have but to acknowledge my lordship and come to a conference." To which the strange man replied: "This is my way, Persian. Neither do I fear men nor flee from them . . . Acknowledge you I do not, but I shall send you appropriate gifts."

The gifts were a bird, a mouse, a frog and five arrows. Questioned about their significance, the bearer suggested that the Persians, if wise, would discover that for themselves.

So the king of kings held a council at which he gave it as his opinion that the items symbolized a Scythian surrender. But his father-in-law, the veteran general Gobryas, found the right answer. His interpretation of the message was roughly this: "Unless, Persians, you can turn into birds and fly into the sky, or become mice and burrow underground, or make yourselves frogs and disappear in the marshes, you will never escape from this land. You will die pierced by arrows." And so, tradition has it, it very nearly came about.

By the time the sixty days had come and gone, Darius and his exhausted soldiers were in disarray, retreating before hordes of harassing Scythians. One band of the enemy rode ahead to the Danube bridge and urged the Greek guards to destroy it and sail off, thereby freeing themselves from the power which ruled over them. This course was keenly seconded by one of the Greek captains, the tyrant of the Thracian Chersonese, that thin strip of land beside the Hellespont now known as Gallipoli.

But the rest of the tyrants were against the proposal, pointing out that their authority depended on Persian patronage. Without Darius, they would be finished. "There is no city," declared the tyrant of Miletus, "that would not prefer democracy." Nevertheless, to satisfy the Scythians, the Greeks dismantled the bridge a bowshot from the north bank and prepared themselves to reassemble it. As it happened, the hard-pressed emperor arrived at the Danube by night to find, as he thought, his hopes of escape gone. In desperation he called from the ranks an Egyptian reputed to possess the loudest voice in the world, and ordered him to shout into the darkness for Greek help. The Greeks heard, the bridge was mended, and the Persians crossed to safety.

Such was the story to emerge after Persia and Greece had become foes—a story in which Greek imagination and prejudice adroitly supplant the imperial success in Thrace with a picture of insane ambition and ignominious failure. It is a cracking good yarn if not taken too literally, and, again, an interesting insight into the Greek mind.

One portion of the story merits particular attention, for it introduces a figure vital to the field of Marathon, now fast approaching, and a fine sardonic edge to the drama. That figure is Miltiades, tyrant of the Chersonese, the man who supposedly favored the destruction of the Danube bridge.

Miltiades was a natural soldier, forceful, energetic and determined. He was also ambitious, high-handed and not unduly scrupulous. His background perhaps explains his autocratic tendencies. His father, Cimon, an Athenian of great wealth and nobility, was a competitive aristocrat known through Greece for his chariot-race victories. Though the family had flourished under the tyranny of Pisistratus, the oppressive Hippias and his brother Hipparchus had counted Cimon on their black list and engineered his murder. This, it might be thought, would have hardened Cimon's son against their tyranny, yet the fact is that Miltiades owed advancement to the murderers. Two of his relatives, an uncle and a brother, had ruled the Greek colony in the Chersonese, and when the latter died, the tyrants supported the installation of Miltiades.

The first act attributed to Miltiades in the province was true

to the absolutist fashion. His brother's rule had been undermined by war and revolt in the settlement. Miltiades lost no
time in asserting his authority. When the principal men of the
Chersonese came to meet him and condole on his brother's
death, he promptly arrested the lot of them. Then, at the head
of a tough corps of mercenaries, he proceeded to stamp his will
on the common flock.

Though a ruler of aggressive discipline, Miltiades could defer
when it suited him. As Persian power extended to the Hellespont, he engaged in no rash sacrifice to pride or independence,
but submitted to the overlordship of Darius, in whose protection his minor tyranny seemed assured. In this, he was no
different from the many vassal tyrants with whom he joined in
providing ships for the Thracian expedition.

That Miltiades had a role at the fateful bridge is not in
question; that which is ascribed him by tradition, however, is
dubious. By the time the story was recorded, Miltiades had
overcome a somewhat ill reputation (of which there will be
more to tell) and was a Greek hero. People demand an appropriate past of their heroes, and will invent it if necessary. It was
necessary that Miltiades should not have been a mere stooge
of Darius. By having him advocate the destruction of the
bridge, he was cleared of that particular inference and became,
moreover, something of a prophetic counselor. For (to play
along with the legend), had the arms of Persia perished at the
Danube, the subsequent invasion of Greece might never have
happened.

There was one conceivable snag to the story. A hero cannot
crudely betray a trust, even if the victim is a Persian. But Greek
ingenuity made short work of that: "If I have not returned after
sixty days, sail home," said Darius; it was, in contractual terms,
the perfect escape clause.

Of course, all this is frail conjecture at the expense of human
dust. Today, few would buy a dog with as little knowledge of
its personal characteristics as we have in our understanding of

any figure in that ancient age. Miltiades *might* have had a vision of Greek destiny, or some imperial dream of his own in Thrace, or simply a grudge against Darius. On the other hand, given the meager evidence, there seems no more reason to accept the distinction between Miltiades and his fellow tyrants, whose interests admittedly were vested in Darius, than there is to accept the Scythian fairyland.

In the end, the fact remains that the emperor, oblivious of the fancies to be stitched upon his campaign, completed the successful subjection of most of Thrace and retired to Asia leaving a mere fraction of his army to tidy up. This detached force, under a general named Megabazus, not only reduced such native tribes and Greek colonies in Thrace as still opposed the empire, but received also the submission of Macedonia.

There was little to raise the hearts of Persia's enemies. With ominous competence, Darius had pushed his boundaries to the very gates of northern Greece.

19 The Rebels

The emperor's chariot rumbled home from Thrace via Sardis,
then by the so-called royal road across the Cappadocian plain
to Comana, through the mountains of Armenia to the Tigris
valley, past the ruins of once mighty Nineveh and south beside
the river lands to Susa.

For the myriad subjects prostrated in his path, Darius blazed
briefly in their midst as a mortal god. Gold earrings glittered
from the royal mane, gold bracelets bound the royal limbs, gold
chains and girdle spanned the richly draped torso. Slaves
fanned the illustrious features with ostrich plumes.

In the royal entourage, lords of seven noble families mingled
with dignitaries of the royal household. Special police, the
king's "eyes and ears," kept a watchful brief as the despot
passed, closely escorted by his hand-picked guards, the "im-
mortals"—black men, brown men and white men of fine physique, hefting short spears distinctively gold-knobbed.

Hard by, marched the columns of seasoned Persian infantry
and jostling, dust-veiled cavalry. "About their heads they had
soft felt caps called *tiaras*, and about their body tunics of
various colours with sleeves, presenting the appearance of iron
scales like those of a fish," observe the Greek writings. "And
about the legs, trousers; and instead of ordinary shields they
had shields of wicker-work, under which hung quivers; and they
had stabbing spears and large bows and arrows of reed, and,
moreover, daggers hanging from the belt at the right thigh."

The people of the wayside, weathered peasants and nomads,
must have watched the procession with hushed respect.
Throughout the world, as they knew it, the emperor's nod was
law; their lives and property stood at his mercy. With the

twitch of a finger, the lofty figure in the chariot could make a
prince of a beggar, or consign a prince to poverty. At the flicker
of an eyebrow, the despot could impose a death sentence—on
the man beside him, or a man two thousand miles distant. And
it was not commonly the best of deaths. Those who offended
the king, or transgressed the criminal code of his empire, were
impaled, thrown into an ash pit to smother slowly, flayed,
buried alive or crucified. The nastier alternatives need not be
dwelt upon, for now Darius had conquest to celebrate, and
doubtless the journey was a festive one.

The royal cooks would have stocked their larders from the
fruitful plains, the royal eunuchs marshaled suitable pleasures
for the tented nights. Persian nobles, for all their high-minded
principles, could not resist the life of luxury. If all power is
corrupting, the immense privilege vested in these few men who
basked in the favor of the king was irresistible. While the mass
of the people ate frugally and thankfully, the ruling class of the
empire feasted fastidious and expensive appetites. They drank
deep, and their harems were replete to superfluity. A senior
wife, or dowager, might achieve influence, but the majority of
wives and concubines—the royal harem housed hundreds—
lived out their sequestered, claustrophobic years largely ignored
by their grand lords.

It was all extraordinarily costly, but then the few moneyed
Persians (there was virtually no Iranian middle class, since
commerce was despised and left to foreigners) could well afford
it. With the dispensation of the emperor, the noble families
which provided his governors and generals assiduously milked
the wealth of the dominions. Their residences, parks and retinues were stately.

Above all, the royal establishment itself was imcomparable.
The most southerly seat of the monarchy was at Pasargadae,
the home of the old tribal chiefs, among low, rounded hills in
the valley of the Polvar, a river flowing into the Persian Gulf.
Forty miles to the north, on the plain of Mervdasht, was the

grander palace of Darius at Persepolis, screened from the Gulf and the Iranian plateau by twin arms of the Zagros Range. North again, on the fringe of the plateau, stood the palace of Ecbatana, founded by the first of the Median monarchs, symbolic of the Aryan union. And, finally, through the mountains to the southwest, the vale of Kerkeh was dominated by the great residence Cyrus had raised at Susa, because—as he had explained with a magnanimity only equaled by historical ignorance—the capital of Elam had lacked its share of past enterprise "and had always been in subjection to other nations."

The maintenance of such places was, in itself, a major enterprise swallowing huge revenues. Swarms of slaves and overseers worked to keep up the palaces, with their massive terraces, bosky "paradises" stocked for hunting parties, gilded walls, flights of columns, imposing halls and audience chambers, colored friezes and bas-reliefs of the empire's multitudinous wonders.

If Persia borrowed freely from the artistry around her, from Babylon, Assyria, Egypt and Hellas, in creating these treasure houses to the glory of the king of kings, the splendors of Darius were none the worse for such borrowing. Persian craftsmen did not copy slavishly. In their architecture, sculpture, cloisonné work, gold jugs and dishes, silver vessels, bronze weaponry and in a wealth of other ornamentation, the great palaces reflected the native touch. The feudal conurbations clustered around them might have seemed squalid to an Athenian citizen. But the court of Darius was unrivaled. Thronged with captains and embassies, chancellors and stewards, heralds, pages and musicians, it cannot but have impressed the grandest of visitors.

One visitor to Susa in the immediate aftermath of the Thracian expedition must now be considered, not so much for the importance of his role in what follows, since that at best is equivocal, but as a reminder of the peculiar difficulties Darius faced in his Greek subjects.

Lumping the Greek colonies of Thrace and Macedonia with those of Asia Minor, it can be said that at least a third of the Greek race had been brought under Persian sway. The usefulness of these people had not been lost on Darius, who had employed their skills and initiative successfully in Europe, but the assets had to be qualified. A corollary of competence is independence, and the exploits of the aforementioned visitor suggested rather irksomely that given an inch, a Greek might take an ample yard.

The man in question was the tyrant of Miletus, Histiaeus, the senior Ionian leader at the Danube bridge. That Darius appreciated his services was evident, for Histiaeus was granted possession of a Thracian town, Myrcinus, after the campaign. It was a thriving place, with good land and silver mines not far away, and the Greek tyrant was soon planning its future. Just what he proposed to do with Myrcinus is a mystery. There has been much speculation. Some have imagined him setting up a base for freebooting operations; others have discerned the nucleus of a more grandiose scheme at Myrcinus, perhaps a projected dominion to rival the authority of Sardis. It is not of great importance. What matters is that Histiaeus aroused the suspicion of the general Megabazus, seemingly by the fortifications he erected, and that Megabazus reported the situation to Darius. The emperor acted suavely. Summoning the suspect to Susa, he announced blandly that the company of his friend Histiaeus was indispensable to the Persian court—and there, in colonnaded luxury, the tyrant was to languish with such permanency that his features became as familiar to the Susanians as the bas-reliefs.

If there was a lesson for Darius in Histiaeus, it was that the Greeks should be watched very carefully.

Remote from Persia, alien to the Asian mentality, the westerners were still something of an unknown quantity in the halls of central government where, after all, they were but a peripheral factor in a vast administrative complex. By and large, responsibility for the outlying affairs of the empire resided with provincial authorities, the bureau at Sardis being relevant to the Greeks. Persia's man in Sardis, a satrap named Artaphernes, was a capable and self-sufficient governor. The tyrants through whom he controlled the Ionian and other Greek subjects of his satrapy treated him with respect, while in his dealings with Greece itself, he pursued an edgy relationship with firmness and a shrewd awareness of the empire's expanding interests.

Imperial policy in the Aegean had hardened since acquiring the Thracian coast. For long enough—ever since the Spartans had presumed to lecture Cyrus—Hellas had treated Persian Asia Minor with some contempt, providing haven and support for those who rejected its regime. The only politicians who came to Sardis prepared to treat deferentially with the satrap were deposed tyrants seeking aid to reinstate themselves.

At last, with the expulsion of Hippias from Athens, Artaphernes resolved to take a tough line. Through the exiled Hippias, and his Pisistratid adherents in Attica, the satrap saw a chance to gain a hold in the Balkan Peninsula. Take back the tyrant, he admonished the Athenians, or beware the consequences. If these words were not explicit, the trend may be deduced with fair confidence, for about the same time Artaphernes dispatched spies to report on the armaments of Hellas. Thus, in about 506 B.C., the ice of what would be thought of today as a cold war began to deepen between Athens and Sardis.

How far Artaphernes consulted with Susa in such matters is problematical. Most likely, he acted freely within a pretty wide brief—gain to Persia being the cardinal principle. On such a basis, he had cause to look west with some complacency. Strategically and materially, he was on firm ground, but there was a less tangible determinant in the reckoning.

Political theories meant little to the mind of an Iranian, for the writ of despotism had run in Asia for as long as civilization, and what is beyond experience is beyond comprehension. For Greece, however, politics offered an alternative peculiarly suited to its native traits—so apposite, indeed, that in many quarters the merits of democracy had become less a conviction than a passion, its irreconcilability with despotism a decree of faith. That passion was about to shake the complacency of Artaphernes with a violence and from an area quite unexpected.

Since its suppression by Cyrus, the democratic sentiment in Ionia had smoldered inconspicuously under the Persian-sponsored tyrants. The Greek ports of Asia Minor had other grievances. The tributes due to Sardis were disagreeable, and the commercial advance of the Phoenicians under the aegis of Darius was resented. But above all, the deprivation of self-government rankled their talented and assertive citizens. In Miletus, the greatest of the cities, the replacement of the absent tyrant Histiaeus by his uninspiring son-in-law, Aristogoras, heightened the climate of ferment. Had Aristogoras stayed put and ruled firmly things might have happened differently, but like his mistrusted relative, he was lured to ill-fated adventure.

The story of Aristogoras begins in a setting of deceptive tranquillity, in Naxos, a green and prosperous plot far from the rival lands to east and west. But Naxos, largest of the central isles of the Cyclades—those sunny stepping stones from Asia Minor to southern Greece—was a vital pawn in the tussle for Aegean ascendancy. Thus its government was of more than local interest.

At about the turn of the century, a democratic rising on this lovely and populous island ousted its ruling oligarchs. The oligarchs fled to Miletus, where Aristogoras, not the least opportunistic of Greek tyrants, contemplated the rewards of restoring them to their former power. The venture was appealing, but Aristogoras was not precipitate. First, he sought the

approval and support of his imperial master at Sardis. Artaphernes needed little instructing in the advantages of a stake
in the Cyclades, and Persian backing was liberal.

Expensively subsidized by the satrap, Aristogoras assembled
an armada and descended on Naxos. For four months, he laid
siege to the capital, but its people, having tasted freedom from
oppression, did not intend to relinquish it easily. Their spirited
resistance, combined, it seems, with a personal feud between
Aristogoras and an admiral provided by the Persians, frustrated
the invasion. The siege was withdrawn and the armada turned
back for Miletus.

Aristogoras must have done some hard thinking on the voyage home. His prospects, rather suddenly, had ceased to be
enviable. His sponsors were not tolerant of failure; the Persian
admiral was in no mood to endorse his apologia. At best, he
could expect to be relieved of his tyranny; at worst, to lose his
life with it.

Fate offered an incongruous way out. On his return, Miletus
was seething with democratic sentiment, ripe for rebellion.
Aristogoras seized his chance with characteristic Greek prag-
matism. Renouncing his title as tyrant, the would-be reducer
of democratic Naxos solemnly proclaimed himself apostle of
the new order. Miletus rose fervently to the gesture. Other
tyrants who had accompanied the armada were arrested in the
harbor. Citizens' representatives were dispatched to spread the
message of freedom along the coast. Revolution spread as a
flame through Ionia.

"Remember the Athenians!"

The so-called Ionic revolt, with its deep appeal to Greek emotion and its immediacy to the struggle at Marathon, spawned some colorful anecdotes.

In one of the best known, the declining Histiaeus is plucked from the stately shadows of Susa, divested of the dust of twelve neglectful years and crowned with a leading role. According to this belief, the exiled tyrant, yearning for his native haunts and prerogatives, instigated the rebellion by sending a trusted slave to Miletus with a message tattooed beneath the hair on his scalp. Having the man shaved, Aristogoras read a call for insurrection and obeyed the will of his father-in-law.

Improbable as this story is, its underlying contention—namely, that Histiaeus anticipated being sent home by Darius to restore order—is supportable. The tyrant was indeed released during the rising, though it did him little good. Neither the provincial administration at Sardis nor the rebels of Miletus trusted him, and he departed, rejected, to the offshore islands, where he spent his last years in piracy.

Conceivably, the traditional account of his revolutionary initiative arose from his efforts to ingratiate himself with the Milesians when the satrap spurned his services. The only certainty attached to the episode is that it characterizes the ambiguity of many a Greek autocrat, especially among the ruling colonials, caught in the crossfire between Persia and democracy. For Histiaeus it led to a grim end. Apprehended in his piratical adventures, he was crucified by Artaphernes.

As a rebel, Aristogoras had an equally bleak career. Sailing to Greece to raise support against the satrap, he received a cool welcome at Sparta. The later tale of his audience is as memorable as that of the tattooed slave.

His scheme, asserts the legend, was to inspire his soldierly hosts with a vision of Asiatic conquest. He had with him a map of the earth, as he knew it, engraved on bronze, describing the prestige and wealth to be won from the Persians. The Spartans, allegedly ignorant of the relevant geography, peered closely at the map, finally inquiring as to the length of the march to Susa. "Three months," replied Aristogoras unguardedly. The discussion closed abruptly. "Be off, Milesian stranger," he was told, "before sunset." It is hard to believe that the cautious Spartans, slow to commit themselves beyond the Peloponnesus at the best of times, would consider Aristogoras seriously. Packing his bag, he moved to Athens.

The Athenians, mindful of their kinship with the Ionians and their argument with Sardis over Hippias, were more sympathetic. Politically the powerful democratic sentiment in the city responded to the rebel cause. Strategically its success was extremely desirable. A line of independent strongholds on the eastern Aegean, culturally and ideologically linked to Athens, was a reassuring prospect. Like the Spartans, however, the Athenians were not so rash as to look for a head-on conflict with Persia, nor, for that matter, were they so free of isolationist tradition as to be whole-hearted about any foreign policy.

After hearing Aristogoras, they agreed to support him with a small fleet, to which their island neighbors, the Eretreans of Euboea, contributed a few ships. The idea seems to have been to encourage rather than to substantially reinforce the rebels.

But, as often happens, meddling proved a painful compromise. In 498 B.C., fortified by the somewhat limited fruits of his recruiting trip, Aristogoras launched a flamboyant and tactically disastrous assault on Sardis. Accompanied by the Athenian contingent, the rebels forced an entrance to the city, but were repulsed at the citadel by the satrap and his guards. Contenting himself with setting fire to the environs, Aristogoras retreated. Between Sardis and the coast, the attackers were intercepted by Persian reinforcements and roughly punished for their temerity. The Athenian party had seen enough to doubt the wisdom of its venture. Taking to its ships, it left Aristogoras to his own devices and sailed home.

But the damage was inflicted. Had Athens deliberately sought to envenom its relationship with Persia, it could scarcely have done so more effectively than by participating in the burning of Sardis under the nose of Artaphernes.

Herodotus dramatizes the fury of Darius in vivid lines: "The Athenians?" rasps the emperor on learning of the incident. "Who are these Athenians?" Then, summoning a palace slave, he commands him to recite three times whenever the king dines: "Master, remember the Athenians!" For Herodotus, the affair is heavy with significance. It was, he contends sweepingly, "the beginning of evil between Greeks and barbarians."

Aristogoras did not wait to finish what he had started. As the Persian counteroffensive mounted, he fled to the shores of Thrace where, debating a further departure, he was killed in a siege near the Macedonian frontier. His death was no great loss to the rebel cause. Popular movements, deriving their impetus from common desires or grievances, seldom lack cynical exploiters, and while it may be doing Aristogoras an injustice to paint his leadership as entirely self-seeking, certainly he did little good for the Ionians.

Apart from quickening the spleen of Darius, the clumsy attempt on Sardis had alienated the native Lydians, whose sympathies were of much importance in the struggle. It had also put an end to any chance of compromise. Hitherto, the regime of the satrap had been lenient; now the Persians were determined to stamp out opposition by any means.

For several years the Ionians fought fiercely for their liberty, yet, as once against Cyrus, with more conviction than cohesion. With the enemy controlling the interior, the coastal cities, isolated by the heights enfolding their sheltered vales, had few tactical options. Again, the Persians were free to pursue a systematic war of sieges.

Only at sea did the Ionians get together in realistic strength, and even then there were disruptive jealousies. In 494 B.C., joined by a squadron from the Aeolian island of Lesbos, the rebel fleet rallied to the relief of Miletus, then invested by a Persian land and naval force. The Lesbians were hardy sailors and stout individualists, but before the Persians were even encountered, the Ionian fleet was at odds over discipline, and desertions were imminent. When the enemy navy appeared, strong in Phoenician, Egyptian and Cypriote squadrons, the distrust among the Greek allies proved catastrophic. Most of the Lesbians, and many others, departed at the crucial moment, and though some fought stubbornly, Persia was handed the victory.

The fate of Miletus was now sealed. Stormed by land and sea, the defenders fell back on the citadel, where they were overwhelmed. Most of the men of the city were slaughtered, the women and children driven into slavery, the buildings ransacked and then destroyed. Thus perished the diadem of Ionia, for though the desolated city was revived at a later date, it never regained its old glory and prosperity.

The ruin of Miletus shocked the Greek world. Athens received the news with special anguish. Some time afterward, when a tragedian named Phrynicus made the fall of the great port the theme of a drama, people were moved to tears, and he was fined for suggesting that the Athenians should have done more for the Ionians.

Meanwhile the Persian fleet scourged the rebel coast toward the Hellespont, while the satrap's armies completed the repression. They did a thorough job. In the words of the ancient historian: "And now the Persian commanders made good the threats they had uttered before battle . . . When they were masters of the cities, they seized the best-looking boys and had them mutilated to serve as eunuchs, and tore the fairest girls from their homes and carried them to the king . . . and, moreover, they burnt the temples and cities. For the third time the Ionians were reduced to slavery: first by the Lydians, twice by the Persians." Small wonder the Athenians preferred not to dwell on the fate of the Ionians. It was all too real to them.

Against the remorseless strength and organization of the empire, the Greeks of Asia Minor had displayed a disunity and ineptitude of leadership which may or may not have surprised Darius, but must surely have enhanced the appeal of westerly expansion.

"Remember the Athenians!" intoned the slave of legend. Darius and his strategists needed no reminding. If Miletus had been the glory of subject Greece, Athens was the golden gate to free Hellas. A bauble, perhaps, beside the treasures of the empire, but a tempting one.

The preoccupation of Artaphernes and the forces of his satrapy with the revolt in Ionia had meant a temporary relaxation of Persian vigilance in Thrace, and the various communities there had reverted to their old ways.

In Macedonia the king renounced his allegiance to the emperor; on the coast between the Bosphorus and the Hellespont, a number of Greek settlements joined the rebellion.

In the Chersonese, the controversial figure of Miltiades looked to his own interests. Unlike Histiaeus—and awkwardly for subscribers to the Danube legend—the standing of Miltiades with the empire had remained unimpaired since the campaign in Thrace. While the eastern Aegean rang to the blows of freedom's battle, the thrustful Miltiades assembled his henchmen and embarked on a private war.

To the west of the Chersonese, two islands, Imbros and Lemnos, offered prospects of enrichment to the acquisitive warrior. That their peoples had recently acknowledged Persian authority did not deter him. His own regime was endorsed by Darius—besides, the satrap had his hands full elsewhere. Miltiades mounted his expedition from Elaeus, the Chersonese port nearest to the islands. It proceeded successfully. Miltiades was no bungling Aristogoras, nor was he inhibited by democratic sentiments. Both Imbros and Lemnos fell to the tyrant, now master of his own modest empire.

The triumph was short-lived. News of the fall of Miletus and the approach of the emperor's fleet, arbitrarily dispensing retribution on the coastal Greeks, forced a tricky decision on the tyro imperialist. He could not match the armaments of the grand fleet. Could he convince its captains, particularly if they were Phoenicians or Cypriots, of his loyalty to Darius? On reflection, he decided against awaiting the answer. Loading five ships with his kin and valuables, he left the Chersonese for his native Athens.

As it turned out, the departure may not have been necessary. One of the vessels, with the tyrant's eldest son, Metiochus, was intercepted by the Phoenicians, who sent their captive to Darius. Far from showing displeasure with the family, the emperor loaded Metiochus with favors and offered him a Persian wife.

Ignorant of his son's fate, Miltiades arrived in Athens and sought out his old friends. But times had changed since the days of Hippias. He had barely settled when he was arrested and placed on trial for tyranny.

The revolt in Ionia had dragged on for six years. Though doomed to failure and savage retribution, it was a portentous struggle, one of the first great risings in history combining a war of independence and a people's revolution.

The rebels had fought with a stubborn and impassioned heroism none the less impressive for the attendant failure of their strategies. Miletus itself had held out for two long years under heavy pressure from superior forces with siege techniques which had reduced mighty bastions in a few weeks.

To many Persians, the rebellion may have seemed of little consequence: just another disturbance duly quelled on distant frontiers. But it had been a costly operation, and for Greeks and the more aware Persians, the episode gave cause for sharp reflection. Large numbers of ships and men had been involved, and the northwestern administration severely disrupted.

In Athens, as elsewhere in Greece, the agony of Ionia appeared as a telling illustration of the capacities of Darius, a grave warning to any man whose mind ranged beyond immediate contingencies.

In the councils of Susa and Persepolis the rebellion was blamed on the failure of the tyrannical system as an adjunct of government at Sardis, and on the subversive influence of free Greece on Greek Asia.

It was the Persians who responded with positive policies. While Athens did its best to forget Miletus, Darius promptly tackled the threefold requirements disgorged by the upheaval: namely, the reorganization of the subject Greeks, the reassertion of control in Thrace and Macedonia, and the furtherance of Persian interests in Greece itself. His approach to these objectives reveals the versatility of the great despot—flexible, subtle, incisive and frankly violent as the turn was called.

It must be remembered that the Aegean was only one of many problem areas for the king of kings. The eastern reaches of the empire were seldom free from crisis; Egypt was a constant source of trouble demanding both tact and the threat of large standing armies; Babylon had its fair share of dissidents.

Darius applied his correctives, sometimes mild, sometimes pitiless, with a canny flair for the apposite, now demonstrated ingeniously in Ionia. The system of ruling the Greeks through tame tyrants had been discredited. Too often the tameness had proved illusory, a mask for grasping and aggressive self-interest. For the most part, admittedly, the tyrants had vented their ambitions on fellow Greeks, but in the end, Sardis had inherited the bitterness.

The Ionians had fought for democratic governments. Having crushed them, Darius resolved to give them the government they wanted. After all, as he probably rationalized, if the rebellion had taught him anything about democracy, it was that it was obligingly divisive. Naturally, democratic government as the emperor envisaged it would be responsible to the satrap—a very limited freedom—but granting it was an astute stroke, a balm to the battered pride of the Ionians and a baited snare for the free Greeks. Within months of bloody and merciless repression, Darius was revising the window of his Aegean emporium with magnanimity and conciliation to the forefront.

The man picked to implement this disarming exercise was from the highest ranks of Persian nobility, a glittering soldier named Mardonius, son of the veteran general Gobryas and recently honored by marriage to a daughter of the king himself. Mardonius arrived on the coast of Asia Minor with a strong body of fresh troops and assumed supreme command not only of the army already in the theater but of a substantial section of the dominions' fleet. He worked quickly. During the spring of 492 B.C., the transformation of local government was completed.

The new system was not entirely charitable. The defeated cities were carefully surveyed to discover what revenues the Persian treasury might expect from them in future, and their military privileges were tightly circumscribed. But at least the reforms patched over the worst wounds of rebellion, allowing Persian ambassadors to approach the cities of free Greece with plausible policies.

At about this time, or soon after, heralds were busy through-out Hellas offering Persian good will and protection in return for recognition of the emperor's authority. In many cases, their persuasiveness was successful. With human relationships, as with physiological malfunctions, a superficial or lesser com-plaint may distract from a more alarming syndrome, and the neighborly animosities of some Greek states appear to have blinded them to the consuming threat of the eastern giant.

Specifically, Aegina, the island rival of Athens in the Saronic Gulf, accepted Persian overtures, perceiving a cure for local ills while ignoring the encroachment of the grand disease. For others, particularly the weaker communities, union with Persia was probably a case of simple prudence. The tortured ghost of Miletus held Hellas in deep fear.

From Ionia, the lordly Mardonius moved north to undertake the second of his father-in-law's western objectives, the recov-ery of Persian Europe. Once more, Persian troops crossed the straits to Thrace and impressed their command on that coun-try. This time, instead of concentrating on the Danube, the main advance was west to Macedonia, whose ruler hastily reaffirmed the earlier submission.

What appears to have been less a campaign than a triumphal progression was marred for Mardonius by two incidents. At one point, warriors of a Thracian tribe, the Brugi, launched a night attack on the Persian camp, causing some confusion and casu-alties. Mardonius himself was wounded before they were beaten off. The other and more compelling misadventure in-volved the supporting fleet which, in customary fashion, was keeping pace with the land force along the coast, the northern rim of the Aegean. Here it suffered a disaster of disputed magnitude upon which hinges an argument of engaging complexity.

One school of thought about the expedition of Mardonius holds that its aim was confined to the reclamation of Thrace and Macedonia, and that Mardonius retired with his mission fully accomplished. The other, following Greek tradition, maintains that the ultimate purpose of the Persian enterprise was to penetrate Greece from Macedonia and attack Athens and Eretria, if not to overbear wider areas of the Balkan Peninsula. According to this theory, the mission was aborted by a storm which wrecked the fleet off Mount Athos, at the tip of Akti, one of three remarkable promontories which jut trident-like into the Aegean south of Macedonia. At this location, the currents are dangerous and the sea often turbulent. It seems that a northeasterly gale swept the cape as the fleet was passing, causing many losses. Herodotus heard an assertion that three hundred ships were destroyed and that twenty thousand men perished, though the figures are extremely improbable and even the ancient account implies skepticism. However, having accepted the premise of a Persian attempt on Greece via Thrace and Macedonia, the Greeks of a later time could only explain the seemingly premature withdrawal of Mardonius by a disaster of some size.

On the whole, it is easier to believe that he had, in fact, accomplished his assignment with the subjection of the former dependencies, and that the loss of the ships was incidental. Certainly, Mardonius is not represented in the annals as a failure. On the contrary, Herodotus portrays him as being thoroughly complacent about his achievements—an acknowledgedly successful general. Subsequent events were to suggest emphatically that Persian naval resources had not been seriously depleted.

While Mardonius spanned the western shores of the empire, Miltiades, the refugee tyrant from the Chersonese, rediscovered his native Athens. When Miltiades had sailed from the city as a younger man, Hippias and Hipparchus were still in power. For as long as he could remember before that, their father, the tyrant Pisistratus, had been the greatest figure in Athenian politics. The democratic regime he now encountered was neither familiar, nor suited, to the style of Miltiades.

Unfortunately, since his confrontation with the system is a fascinating and crucial feature of our narrative, knowledge of the political groupings in democratic Athens is both imprecise and notoriously difficult to summarize.

The old factions of coast, plain and hill had become blurred before Miltiades had left for the Chersonese. Clans and family followings now provided a sharper focus on political rivalry. For some time the Alcmaeonid clan, which had given Athens the great reformer Cleisthenes, had led the democratic movement. Among opposition factions were the Pisistratids, adherents of the former tyrants, and their enemies of the reactionary Philaid clan, once headed by Cimon the aristocrat, father of Miltiades. On a broader scale, such economic and class divisions as the nobility, the commercial families and the mass of poorer citizens had the makings of parties, or pressure groups, in the loosest sense.

Athenian politics, a constantly shifting permutation of alliances and transformations, is none the clearer to the distant observer for the impersonal, not to say ephemeral, style of the democratic executive. When one man rules absolutely, as in Persia, an understanding of the man is a measure of the government. When the government is every man, and many take a turn in its councils, illuminating figures are less evident.

Oddly enough, the simplest guide to Athenian politics at this time can be obtained by a glance at the area of their least efficiency, namely the foreign field.

A quick return to the expulsion of Hippias is necessary. When tyranny was overthrown and Cleisthenes, at the head of the Alcmaeonids, laid the formal foundations of democracy, the foreign area that obsessed the democrats had been Sparta.

Sparta was strong and Sparta was conservative. It will be remembered that the Spartan king, Cleomenes, was resolved to crush the popular movement he had reluctantly abetted in Athens and to restore the power of the aristocrats. Scarcely on its feet, Athenian democracy was threatened with extermination by the combined forces of the west and the reactionaries in its midst.

In the desperation of the moment, Cleisthenes turned east for help, to Persia. It was importuning the devil, and the devil named a high price. At Sardis, the democratic embassy was informed that Persian protection depended on Athens pledging homage to Darius, whereupon, in the words of Herodotus, "the envoys accepted the terms on their own responsibility, but, on returning to Athens, fell into deep disgrace for their compliance."

Shortly afterward, the Athenian assembly repudiated the action of the envoys. Nevertheless, at this point the Alcmaeonids appeared in the light of the Medizing, or Persian-oriented, party, while the aristocrats were pro-Spartan.

This situation was modified by two events: the Spartan league against Athens collapsed with the withdrawal of Corinth; and the exiled Hippias took refuge at Sardis. With the restoration of the tyrant explicit in Persian policy, it had become political suicide for the Alcmaeonids, or any democratic Athenian, to continue to court the east. From now on, there could be only one Medizing party in Athens—the Pisistratids, the party of Hippias.

At the same time, the democrats were not so confident as to throw discretion to the winds, and a reluctance to exasperate the great eastern power became evident with the rebellion in Ionia. Though a majority of Athenians voted for aiding the rebels, the limited character of that aid, both in weight and duration, suggests a delicate balance in the assembly.

Clearly, the Pisistratids would not have supported operations against Sardis, but as they were a minority, and the aristocratic faction probably voted against them, democratic opinion must have been divided, arguably with the artisan class opposed to shedding its blood on distant shores, and the commercial class in favor of sustaining its Ionian contacts. For several years, Ionia remained a divisive and emotional issue, with Athenian society polarized into pro- and anti-interventionists.

As the Persian counteroffensive mounted, interventionist fervor dwindled. Indeed, by 496 B.C., when the ultimate result was beyond doubt, the pressure to reach accommodation with Persia was so strong that a Pisistratid candidate was elected to the high office of archon. Today, it might perhaps be called a protest vote, a warning that the people were sick and tired of war talk.

Hippias must have received the news gleefully. To the despotic mentality, the gusts and eddies of free expression are deceptive, and if Sardis read too much into the event it would not have been the last time in history that a totalitarian regime was misled by democratic fickleness.

Within two years, the sack of Miletus and the terrible fate of the Ionians had once more swung the balance of Athenian politics. In a wave of popular revulsion the Pisistratid archon disappeared, and in his place rose a new type of Greek leader, a man of the middle class, a man whose background lacked either wealth or distinction.

Themistocles was to emerge as one of the most capable statesmen of ancient Greece, and though his fame was to come after Marathon, already his farsightedness and political dexterity were manifest. His appeal was strong in trading and industrial circles, among the self-made people who had stimulated democracy in the first place. He must also have attracted many of the younger, unestablished citizens who might once have gravitated to the Alcmaeonids. He was not, if Plutarch is correct, a very cultured man.

This novel leader believed in an outgoing Athens, an expanding future. He was excited by maritime prospects. He planned a new naval harbor at Piraeus. He backed rugged champions of worldly experience, and was more interested in their usefulness to himself and the state than in their finer sentiments.

With a ruthless streak of his own, he understood forceful men. By a fateful coincidence, Miltiades arrived in Athens at the very moment the star of Themistocles began to shine.

Since the murder of Cimon, the Philaid clan had not been prominent in Athenian politics. The loss of its energetic and aristocratic chief, the departure of his son Miltiades for the Chersonese, the rise of its rivals, the Alcmaeonids—each of these had helped to weaken the Philaids.

Now the return of Miltiades, an experienced ruler and soldier in the prime of life, must have stimulated visions of revival among his father's people. Home at last was the noble son, the sea-tanned venturer. Might not Miltiades, untainted by democratic heresies, lead them, perhaps even Athens, to better things?

Though the Philaids and, doubtless, many aristocrats may have reasoned this way, others took a different view. The Pisistratids had not eliminated Cimon to see another Philaid covet the empty palace to which Hippias would return when the time was right. Nor can the mass of democrats have been enthralled by the sudden reappearance of this autocratic figure, last seen setting sail with tyrannical blessing in a warship provided by his father's murderers.

Some of the Athenians, almost certainly Alcmaeonids, lost

no time expressing their distaste. He had barely landed, so
tradition has it, when "his enemies brought Miltiades before
a court of law and prosecuted him for his tyranny in the
Chersonese." The charge was a grave one, with death as a
possible penalty.

Yet the trial is lost to posterity. Of its proceedings, not a fact
is reported saving the verdict—an exasperating if understand-
able omission by the ancients, for the wrangle must have riv-
eted its own day, and in hindsight, becomes one of the most
extraordinary judicial conflicts in history.

It is not hard to imagine the case brought against Miltiades
by the democrats. The accused had been appointed to the
Chersonese as an agent of the Pisistratid tyranny, he had ruled
as an autocrat, and he had imposed his sway by force, not only
over the promontory but on the people of Imbros and Lemnos.
Moreover, he had compounded his tyranny by placing it at the
service of Persia. The accused had held a command in the
Thracian expedition of Darius, and his family had been honored by the emperor. Then there was his behavior during the
Ionic rebellion. Far from concording with the ideals of the
Ionians, Miltiades had exploited the struggle for self-interest,
enlarging his personal empire at the expense of Greek islanders.
What did such a man want in democratic Athens if it was not
to raise a new tyranny? And what did democratic Athens want
with such a man?

The case *for* Miltiades is not difficult to postulate, for his
apologists have been arguing it throughout history. The defendant's father had been assassinated by the Pisistratid tyrants. To
call the son's rule an extension of their tyranny was to fly in
the face of human nature, and to deny the bitterness between
Pisistratid and Philaid. The defendant had served with the
Persians only against distant barbarians, and (if it can be assumed that the Danube bridge story was introduced at this
point) had been the least cooperative of the emperor's Greek
captains. As for the Ionic revolt, while the Ionians were losing

to the Persians, the defendant had actually gained ground from the empire. Imbros and Lemnos had deferred to Sardis before he had invaded them. He had seized the islands as an Athenian, for Athens. Indeed, he had been driven from the Chersonese by the forces of the empire—the same empire which sought to reimpose Hippias on the Athenians. As a Philaid, and the son of a noble Athenian, he earnestly opposed the party of Hippias.

Legally, the case appears to have rested on a finer point. According to Herodotus, the charge was "tyranny in the Chersonese." Since that could hardly mean tyranny over the natives, who were not the concern of Attic law, it must have meant over Athenian nationals in the settlement. Strictly speaking, therefore, the issue would appear to have depended on the evidence of such of these who may have fled the Chersonese with, or prior to, Miltiades. History reveals nothing of such people. What it does reveal, and probably to more point, is that the case was political, and that political trials at any period are not resolved primarily on legalities.

That is not to suggest that the court was rigged in any crude sense. It would have been very difficult to bribe or coerce a substantial portion of the several hundred citizens who would judge such a case and whose identities were unknown until the morning of the session.

Yet the very size of the jury, allied to the political consciousness of the Athenian citizen, played into the hands of the popular leadership. There can be little doubt that as the democratic favorite of the moment, Themistocles had considerable influence over the court's vote.

In other circumstances, this must have sealed the doom of Miltiades. But Themistocles was no slave to doctrinaire postures. Miltiades may well have struck him as too useful a man to sacrifice on the democratic altar, whatever his prosecutors thought of him. Faced with the combined menace of the Persians and Hippias, there was much to be said for a détente between the democrats and the aristocrats. Miltiades could be the vital link. Furthermore, his aggressive military record and his intimate knowledge of Persian arms, war psychology and tactics were assets too timely to be overlooked by the practical Themistocles.

At all events, Miltiades was acquitted. Nor did his good fortune end there. The same year, he was promoted to the board of Athenian generals.

23 The Armada

In the summer of 490 B.C. one of the greatest armadas then seen assembled at Samos, off the coast of Ionia. Long, sleek warships littered the sunny shores in dark shoals. Men of a dozen nations—bronzed Levantines, superior Persians, tough Medes, Syrians, Cilicians, Cypriotes—busied themselves with last-minute adjustments to vessels and armaments. Darius was ready to teach Athens and Eretria that the empire was not assailed with impunity.

And yet, while the emperor called for vengeance, the blow was born of a deeper certainty. Sooner or later, the Greeks of Europe had been bound to defend themselves or succumb to the Persian giant. There was no room for freedom on the fringe of a swelling despotic world.

The only unpredictable feature of the advance west was the chosen nature of the master stroke: a quick seaborne uppercut rather than a long, looping land punch. It suggests that Darius was not seeking to reduce Greece at a single thrust but to paralyze Attica, put in his tyrant, then use the bridgehead to conquer the Peloponnese and central states afterward.

The method had pointed validity. By a major amphibious operation, albeit a novelty in the annals of Persian war, the king could put his troops straight on to their objectives without the losses implicit in a circuitous campaign through northern Greece.

But there were drawbacks. One was the character of the ancient warship. Evolved from raiding vessels and fast, pirate-evading traders carrying small cargoes of high value, the Mediterranean galley of the day was notable for mobility rather than capaciousness.

Of sophisticated construction—planks attached to an internal framework, with keel, stem and sternpost—these ships were narrow, shallow and elegant, fitted with a sharp ram-bow and sweeping stern. A single sail was set on a yard slung horizontally from a short mast, but the main source of propulsion was oar power. In this, the warships of Greece and the Persian empire were well-endowed.

Once, about the time of the Trojan wars, the normal galley had been a fifty-oared vessel with a single row of twenty-five oars on either side. Then more power had been called for. But the ship could not be extended to seat a longer line of oarsmen without weakening the back of the slender craft, already vulnerable to what seamen call "hogging" and "sagging" strains. So a double-banking system of oars had been introduced, the rowers staggered so that the oars of the upper bank just missed the heads of the lower bank. This produced the so-called bireme. And the bireme was superseded by the trireme, with yet a further bank of oarsmen in a vessel not much larger than the single-bank galley. Just how all these rowers crammed into the trireme is something of a mystery. It appears that oars of differing lengths were used to facilitate interjacent seating.

At any rate, the outcome was conspicuous: the trireme—in standard commission by the time of Marathon, and perfected by the Phoenicians who dominated the Persian fleet—was occupied largely by its propulsive crew. Of a normal complement of about two hundred men, the oarsmen outnumbered the warriors by at least three to one. This meant that a very large fleet was needed to transport an army, while room for food, water and sleeping aboard was minimal. Frequent landings were necessary for eating and resting. It was also important to be able to make shore quickly in rough weather, for, though fast and maneuverable, the galleys were unsafe in heavy seas.

The route Darius approved for the armada—via the Cyclades to Eretria, on the long island of Euboea off Attica, then across the strait to mainland Greece and Athens—was admirably suited to an ancient fleet, for the longest reach between possible landings was not much more than thirty miles. Beyond Naxos, there would be an island every ten miles or so. If the desert warriors of Iran were apprehensive of this new mode of transport, the ships' captains were confident.

The sight from the headlands of Samos as the fleet stood out from the big island, picked up its formations and made west must have lingered in local memory for decades. Tradition puts the number of triremes at six hundred. Since the same figure occurs in accounts of other campaigns involving fleets of the empire, it may be a rational estimate of the resources of Persia's maritime subjects in the eastern Mediterranean. On the other hand, it may be no more than a symbol for the empire's naval fecundity.

Statistical uncertainty is fundamental to the action now unfolding; nevertheless the squadrons trailing their wakes toward the land of gods and heroes must have contained several hundred of those graceful ships.

It may also be fair to assume there were less powerful war craft in the great force, for though Herodotus speaks only of triremes it would be a singular navy whose vessels were entirely of one class. Small coastal communities, poorer than their neighbors, may still have favored biremes, or galleys with fewer oars. And there were the broader and bulkier transporters, more dependent on sail than the warships. Clumsy in combat conditions and vulnerable to ramming, they were not used as troop carriers, but they may have been laden with horses.

It is not hard to imagine the squadrons tightening, weaving geometric patterns on a smooth sea, oars creaking, tossing the warm brine, galleymasters shouting the striking time. Ahead, the flagships spearpointed a foaming trail.

Unusually, two generals shared the supreme command, accompanied by the aging but now inspirited Hippias. Mardonius, perhaps disabled by the wound he had received in Thrace, was not with the armada. The joint leadership had been entrusted to a Mede named Datis, and to the son and namesake of Artaphernes, the Persian satrap of Sardis.

It was a combination of military expertise and political knowledge. Datis, a veteran officer of the breed that had shattered Nineveh, may have been prominent in the repression of Ionia, possibly at Miletus. Artaphernes the Younger was from the noble class of Mardonius; a nephew of the emperor and son of a powerful administrator, he was doubtless well informed by his father on the politics of the Aegean Islands.

Once in Attica, Hippias would provide military intelligence and political influence. Pisistratid agents had kept in contact with him at Sardis. Herodotus had heard that they were at Susa, too.

The omens were good. The armada plowed on past the straggling island of Icaros, or Icaria, white-fringed in a brilliant sea, toward its first landfall, Naxos. Though individual triremes could average eight miles an hour in fair conditions, a fleet holding station by its slowest components was unlikely to average more than five miles an hour. By this reckoning, the journey between the isles was about eight hours.

The shores of Naxos were deserted. It is eloquent of the strength of the swarming squadrons, and the reputation of Persian troops, that the democratic Naxians, having stood resolutely against the arms of Aristogoras, now abandoned their city and fled to the nearby hills.

Datis and Artaphernes exacted grim retribution for the earlier failure. When the capital had been sacked and burned, and its people harassed into submission, a contribution to the armada was exacted from the neighboring island of Paros.

The host then steered north to the little outcrop of Delos, famed for its religious sanctuary. Again, the citizens fled, leaving their homes and temple to the invaders. But the Persian command was too well versed in the Darian philosophy of reward as well as punishment to show a brutal hand everywhere.

Naxos had been used to demonstrate Persian might; Delos was the stage for compassion, for the message that those who had not offended need not fear. Anchoring offshore, the generals paid homage at the altar of the Delian god, and left the island unharmed.

Two centuries later a necklace of twisted gold still lay in the temple, where Datis had left it as a token of good will.

Leaving Delos, the bounding triremes hounded northwest through the Cyclades, levying contingents of troops and taking hostages from the islands on their course, until they reached the southernmost point of Euboea. Here the fine city of Carystus nestled deep in a sheltered bay. The Carystians were friends of their northern neighbors the Eretrians, and on good terms with the Athenians across the Gulf of Petalioi. With obstinate courage, they refused to yield hostages to the Persians or to join the punitive purpose of the great armada. They paid the penalty. Their lands were ravaged, the city beleaguered until it bowed to the eastern sword.

The Persian fleet, its personnel refreshed and sustained on Euboean victuals, now rested in the bay of Carystus. Athenians and Eretrians alike had received reports of its progress with growing consternation. But they could not determine its plans with certainty.

Lying a mere morning's sail from either of their cities, the armada might strike in any direction: southwest across the gulf for Piraeus and Athens, due west for the east coast of Attica, or north into the strait between Greece and Euboea for Eretria. Invincible in western memory, now triumphant throughout the Aegean, the forces of the empire were poised at the gates of the free world. All each city could do was hold its walls and wait for the next move.

It was probably on the fifth of the lunar month of Boedromion, or sometime in September, that the leading triremes nosed out from Carystus and swung their prows north for the narrowing neck of the deep gulf. On the shores, Greek observers raced to spread the warning. Eretria was the target.

The city was small, even by the standards of Greek states, but its people resolved to fight, calling upon Athens for urgent help. Some controversy attaches to the response of the Athenians. It seems that an emergency assembly voted to send the aid requested, but however this was intended, it failed to materialize. Herodotus asserts that orders were dispatched to Chalcis, an Athenian settlement on Euboea, to join the defense of Eretria. That, in fact, the Chalcidians ignored the instruction and fled north, away from their threatened neighbors, is traditionally ascribed to their understanding that the Eretrian leadership was planning treachery.

Whether or not this is taken as an excuse for the Athenian settlers, it has to be accepted that indeed the city had sold out. After a brave defense of several days, the Eretrians were betrayed by a clique of prominent citizens who let in the enemy. The invaders needed no more help. In accord with the wishes of Darius, the temples were pillaged and destroyed in part-revenge for the raid on Sardis, the inhabitants rounded up and impounded for future deportation and slavery.

Athens had been served clear warning of its intended fate. The Persians stayed in Eretria a short while to enjoy the fruits of conquest and prepare for the climax of their triumphant campaign. Then the triremes breasted the strait again. It was a short trip. With Hippias to supervise navigation, the squadrons stood south, Mount Parnes tall to starboard, heading for Marathon.

Eager eyes viewed the first landfall on mainland Greece. A peaceful bay, a gently shelving beach, a broad plain beyond—an invader's dream.

Part 4

A Time for Heroes

Mountains above, Earth's, Ocean's plain below; Death in the front, Destruction in the rear! Such was the scene . . .
    —Byron, *Childe Harold*

Aeschylus, "the founder of drama," was thirty-five in the year of Marathon, the year true drama eclipses the fiction of Greek theater. With his brother, Cynaegirus, the tragedian had watched the glow of danger ripen with each inferno—Naxos, Carystus, Eretria; the reports grow more lurid: gutted temples, slaughtered garrisons, people enslaved and deported.

Now, with the destroyers at Marathon, the brothers took their place in the Athenian militia. To Aeschylus that storm-burdened summer the extinction of Athens cannot have been difficult to visualize. The torch of destruction was just twenty-two miles away. Yet not even Aeschylus could have projected the implications of such a tragedy.

Athens at the time was remarkable for the men of talent it nurtured and those soon to be born. Sophocles was then a child in the city. Sophroniscus, the well-connected citizen who was to sire Socrates, was probably already consorting with the philosopher's mother, Phaenarete.

The chain reaction of potential loss to man's intellectual heritage attendant upon a conquest of Athens that summer, with the resulting slaughter and deportation, is beyond estimation. Without Socrates, what of Plato, assuming his aristocratic forebears survived a Persian victory? And without Plato, what of Aristotle? The loss to western philosophy of Plato alone— the absence of his concern with a rational moral philosophy, his intellectual pursuit of the true scale of virtue, his vision of the soul, the whole metaphysic implicit in his doctrines—is inconceivable.

Even if these, and many other outstanding individuals, are disregarded on the assumption that time and changed circumstance would have reproduced their kind in another skin, it is difficult to dismiss the general climate, the extraordinary surge of social inspiration riding on the outcome of Marathon.

Politically, the mood ran strongly for freedom. Democracy had its opponents, of course, not least among Greek intellectuals. But then, as now, their ability to register dissent and, with few exceptions, to flourish, marked the peculiar merit of the system for a thoughtful and articulate people.

The aims of Greek democracy were clearly recognized. "The most pure democracy," it was written more than two thousand years ago, "is that which is so called principally from that equality which prevails in it, for this is what the law in that state directs: that the poor shall be in no greater subjection than the rich, nor that the supreme power shall be lodged with either of these, but that both shall share it.

"For if liberty and equality, as some persons suppose, are chiefly to be found in a democracy, it must be so by every department of government being alike open to all . . . as the people are a majority and what they vote is law."

It was a blueprint elitists and autocrats would dispute a millennium, two millenniums, later. By the standards of the Persian empire, it was sheer fantasy. "The poor shall be in no greater subjection than the rich"—it was like saying that the starving would be no hungrier than the well-fed! There would be precious little power-sharing anywhere if Athens fell.

As Darius perhaps saw more clearly than most Greeks, with Athens cracked the wedge would be planted for the final hammer-blow at free Greece. When that came, oriental despotism would have burst the last barrier to the west; Europe would lie exposed.

For many days the people of Athens had lived in the shadow of crisis, arms mobilized, ears cocked for the trumpets which would sound the emergency assembly. No need in those edgy hours for the ruddled rope. At the first clamor, the citizens would stop work and converge beneath the sun of late summer on a thronged Pnyx to hear the latest news from the council. When it came, it was stunning. The Chalcidians had fled, Eretria had fallen, the host of the empire was heading for Athens. Prayers and supplications would have to be short.

At this critical moment, the Athenians, like many another community faced with disaster, appear to have shelved their domestic differences and stood united in defiance of the enemy. Arguably, the Persian commanders, through the uncompromising harshness of their punitive acts in Eretria, had themselves to blame, at least in part, for this new political development. Perhaps by now Datis and Artaphernes were complacent. If a degree of political discretion had seemed prudent at the outset of the expedition, it must have lost significance as city after Greek city had collapsed in the path of the armada.

At all events, so far as Athens was concerned, the implications of the Persian treatment of Eretria made it very doubtful if any Greek party could benefit from an eastern triumph. Those Pisistratids who might have welcomed Hippias in his own right must have been much less sure of the tyrant surrounded by a vengeful foreign army. Equally, those Alcmaeonids who might have condoned the crushing of the middle-of-the-road Athenian majority by an outside agency could hardly countenance such a thing at the price the Persians had exacted in Euboea.

In short, while the possibility of isolated conspiracy could not be ruled out, the Athenian fear of a substantial party betrayal had miraculously disappeared. This is clear from the decision of the assembly on learning of the landing at Marathon: one of the most fateful decisions ever taken by a democratic government in ancient Greece. It was to advance and engage the Persians at their point of invasion, rather than to sit tight and try to hold the city. If this seems, at first sight, a less than momentous choice, four points are perhaps worth considering:

1. The invaders had a daunting numerical advantage.

2. The Persians were deemed invincible in the field by most people. According to Herodotus, the Greeks had never stood their ground against a Persian army.

3. Almost every land engagement of the Ionian rebellion and the Persian advance in the Aegean had shown that the Greeks preferred to defend themselves in their cities, not in the open.

4. Originality is rare in the history of warfare, and the idea of a heavily outnumbered force advancing against an accomplished aggressor must have seemed an extraordinary innovation to the ancient Greeks.

Indeed, the plan must have taken some eloquent pleading. While it is not possible to be sure of the source of inspiration, it appears fairly certain that Miltiades was a leading advocate of the strategy. He had established a considerable following in Athens since his court acquittal and elevation to the board of generals, and his authority on Persian war techniques could not be challenged. It is true he had many enemies, both among ultra-conservatives and democrats, but few could deny his capacities in the art of violence—and violent were the hours ahead. Significantly, Miltiades had never waited for the action to come to him. Aggression, unashamed and unexpected, was his hallmark.

The arguments for marching on Marathon made sense. Yet it must be emphasized against the later calumnies of party propaganda that none would have been credible had not Athens overwhelmingly valued freedom above factional interests. The knowledge of an organized fifth column in the city would surely have stopped the army from leaving. Since, however, its departure was an acceptable option, the main ground against an urban defense was the Persian skill in siege warfare. Cities of far greater defensive reputation than Athens had failed to resist the empire, many falling, like Carystus and Eretria, in a few days. Once Athens was invested, relief from Sparta might be too late.

Philippides the runner had been dispatched to summon

Spartan aid. If the city could be screened long enough for the army of the southwestern state to come up (the procrastination of Sparta was yet unknown), a combined front would appreciably lessen the odds on Persia. At the same time, the choice of routes from Marathon to Athens made it impossible to cover the approaches effectively. The only way was to go the whole hog: check the foe at his beachhead. After all, if there was one thing the Persians would not expect, it was to meet the Athenians at Marathon. The shock might deflate their initiative.

Plainly, it is easier to extol the advantages of originality than to put them to the test in a tight corner. In mortal crises, men, like lesser animals, tend to stick to conservative reactions. Characteristically, Athens took the inventive course. Leaving the shelter of their hold, the few marched bravely to challenge the many.

25 Confrontation

The citizens' army of Athens crossed the Attic plain in ten tribes, each with its own strategoi, or general, heading east for the hills between Hymettus and Pentelicus.

Coiling in a dusty column through the dry scrub, through thorny phrygana, asphodel and hyacinth, the army numbered perhaps rather less than a thousand in each tribe: about nine thousand in all, from smooth-skinned youths to desiccated and aging men. To describe their progress as marching, in the strict sense, would hardly be accurate. More likely they traveled in loose bands, without trying to keep step or station, each citizen accompanied by an attendant bearing his weapons and armor. Since there was no organized commissariat in the Athenian army, the men supplied their own provisions: some meal in a knapsack, with salt, garlic and other popular seasonings.

It was a very democratic fighting force. Apart from the overall chief of operations, the polemarch, or war leader, there were just three grades of warriors: generals, colonels (ten of each) and the rest. Disciplines and formalities as modern armies know them did not exist. Merchant and clerk, architect and mason, rich and poor rubbed shoulders with the familiarity of equal rank.

Unlike the Spartans, the Athenians had no full-time army, but they were by no means incompetent when it came to war. At eighteen, every young man of Athens took an oath of honorable military conduct and began a period of hard training in battle drill, skill at arms and physical exercise. From now until he was sixty he would be liable for service at any time; desertion or cowardice could lead to loss of citizenship. After would fill the rear ranks in an engagement, or maybe stand apart and sling missiles at the enemy.

Now they and their comrades pushed briskly through the evergreens of the foothills, intent on reaching Marathon without delay, for it was possible the Persians might avoid them by advancing quickly on another route. Two approaches were open to the enemy. Either he could detour south by the so-called main road, or he could pick a shorter path directly west through the mountains and tolerate a rougher track.

As it happened, the Persians had not moved from Marathon, and the Athenians, drawing close, sought the safety of the adjacent hills. By gaining the slopes in the southern region of the lowlands adjoining the landing beach, they would be able to challenge egress by the main road head-on, at the same time commanding a flanking position should the Persians advance from the shore toward the mountainous western tracks. In this situation—more precisely, perhaps, on the incline of Mount Agrieliki, which dominates the southern aspect of the coastal plain—the citizens halted and surveyed the scene which lay below them.

Bordered on the right by the bay, on the left by the mountains, notably the peaks of Kotroni and Stavrokoraki, the grassy flats stretched north for several miles, terminating at length in broad marshlands. Halfway up the plain, a swift stream, the Charadra, tumbled from the hills in the vicinity of the modern village of Marathon and poured toward the sea across the open ground. This was an arena of appropriately wild grandeur upon which the retinues of war had impressed themselves.

Along the bright rim of the beach, lapped by the ruffles of a drowsy sea, the triremes and transports of the empire wallowed in hostile shoals. Nearby, the plain swarmed with restless easterners, making camp, unloading vessels, riding off in groups to spy and to forage.

The general scene takes no great imagining. Only in statistical terms is the image obstinate. Herodotus gave no estimate a probationary period—probably on garrison duty, frontier pa trol, or building and fortifying outposts—the young militiama became a fully fledged hoplite, or infantryman.

Greece was not, on the whole, a horse-soldier's country, and the Athenians took no cavalry to Marathon. Accustomed to hilly terrain and craggy passes, the Greeks put their faith in those heavily armed footmen whose heroic images are familiar to every Western schoolchild.

The Athenian hoplite supplied his panoply at his own expense, and though not a regular uniform, the components were fairly standard from man to man. On the upper part of the body, he wore a corselet of leather plated with gleaming bronze. This fitted in two halves, laced up the front, and was supplemented with protective shoulder flaps. From the waist down, a short skirt of tough leather thongs, joined to the corselet with a heavy belt, protected hips, abdomen and upper thighs. The top part of the legs was left free of impediment, but padded bronze greaves on the lower part stretched from knee to ankle. The whole outfit was topped by a splendid bronze helmet, the piece, above all, in which the citizen soldier displayed his bravura and elegance. Most helmets were peaked at the front, maybe with a nose guard, and tailed off in a swooping neck-piece. Cheek plates which could be raised or lowered were popular, while decorative chasing graced the realy pretentious headgear. Its crowning glory was the great crest which rose majestically above the brow to conclude in a tail at the soldier's back.

The Greek hoplite wore a short sword at his left side. He also carried into action an ashwood lance tipped with steel. A bronze shield completed all this impressive equipment, sometimes round, sometimes oval, ornamented with animal or mythological devices, and, often, colored tassels.

Not everyone could afford such costly trappings. One citizen might possess part of the armor, another no more than a sword and spear. These more than usually vulnerable individuals of the size of the Persian army, and later figures, mere guesses in hundreds of thousands, are valueless. The one clue of possible worth is the traditional six hundred triremes, which with, at most, fifty warriors to each ship, gives a maximum of thirty thousand fighting men. The figure is much smaller than was once thought, but earlier calculations may have included the crews of the warships. By this reckoning, the number might be raised by about ninety thousand, though with very little relevance, for, like the servants who accompanied the Greek warriors, the oarsmen of ancient fleets were slaves with no effective role as combatants.

Nevertheless, considering the troops of the original armada together with those impressed in the islands, it seems safe to say that the invading army outnumbered the Athenians by between two and three to one. Moreover, a high proportion of the easterners were regular professionals, many hardened veterans and all at least seasoned in the conquests on Euboea.

The imperial troops of the empire, the native Persians, far surpassed the militia of Athens in organization. Herodotus explained that the Persians fought in tens, or multiples of ten, with the army divided into major units of ten thousand, known as myriads. The myriad, subdivided into thousands and hundreds, was commanded by the myriarch, his subordinate officers declining to the dekarch, or leader of ten men.

For the most part, the Persians were lighter in armor than the ancient Greeks. While men of rank, and some special units, wore helmets and padded corselets covered with metal scales, and Persian guardsmen sported boots (a refinement unknown to the Greek soldier), the large number of eastern warriors who went into battle without protective armor amazed the men of Hellas.

But then, the Persians virtually settled many of their battles at a distance. Their classic weapon was the bow, which the footmen used behind a wicker shield, or gerrhon, set up in the ground as a screen against enemy arrows. Their cavalrymen were skilled at shooting from horseback. Effectively flighted, Persian arrow-fire could win an engagement before the two sides came to grips.

For hand-to-hand fighting, the Persians used daggers and short spears, with swords and axes occasionally wielded by horsemen. Normally, the Iranians made great use of mounted troops, but the difficulties of transporting horses by sea in ancient times were considerable, and the ratio of cavalry to foot in the invasion force must have been abnormally low. There were plenty of animals to be had in Euboea, but there could hardly have been shipping space for more than a thousand, if as many.

The armada may have included some Bactrians and Sakai, splendid horsemen who always fought well for the emperor, though the extent of colonials in the force is debatable.

Two factors—the limitation of numbers by the amphibious nature of the expedition, and the extreme competence of its advance from Samos—suggest that only the cream of the emperor's armed resources was utilized: that is, the Persian regulars themselves, plus their brothers-in-arms the Medes, and perhaps the Elamites, those warlike tribes which had once exasperated Assyria and Babylon.

At the same time, if such colonials as the Ethiopians, Egyptians, Hyrcanians and others were not present in force, they were almost certainly represented in smaller numbers. Individuals of outstanding personal prowess were recruited into the imperial regiments from all over the empire.

It was, then, an awesome and exotic scene which met the gaze of the Athenian militiamen; not exactly one to inculcate confidence. Below them in that sprawling camp on the sandy plain teemed the vanquishers of Croesus, Nebuchadnezzar, Psammeticus; the captors of great civilizations and tamers of wild hordes; the masters alike of east and west, of nine-tenths of the known world. If reputations were infallible, Athens was already lost.

Apprehensively, the citizens crouched on the hillside. To a man, they must have prayed Godspeed for Philippides.

26 The War Council

For a time, Athenian and Persian watched each other like cat and dog. Days passed. Nights passed. In the ranks of the militia, older bones must have ached sorely from the chill nocturnal hours on that lofted perch; hearts yearned for dawn and the return of September's sun. Then the wild surrounds would reemerge in fresh brilliance: the crescent bay, rugged limestone mountains, the pines, olives and cedars, scented myrtle and arbutus . . . And still the hostile host on the plain below.

The exact date the Athenians arrived at Marathon is uncertain, but they had departed Athens after Philippides left for Sparta on the seventh of the lunar month, perhaps reaching the coast on the ninth or tenth. The earliest they could expect the Spartans was the thirteenth. Meanwhile they could only wait for a Persian move.

Their position was well chosen. Datis, commanding the invaders on Attic soil, was unlikely to try to storm the difficult rising ground, nor could he move his army from the beachhead without giving an advantage to the watchful Greeks.

In more ways than one, the result was an impasse. Not only were the Persians in favor of fighting on the plain, the broad flats which suited their tactics, but like the Greeks, they had an incentive to procrastinate.

While the Athenians hopefully tarried for the Spartans, the Persian puppet Hippias was pleased to have the time needed to make contact with his agents. Athens empty of troops was a tempting location for treachery. The longer the militia remained at Marathon, the more chance had the tyrant to hatch a conspiracy. For the moment, therefore, both sides regarded inertia without dismay.

It was not until Philippides returned from Laconia with the news that the Spartans refused to march until the full moon that the situation changed, and changed dramatically.

From all Greece the Athenians had received but one gesture of solidarity. For some years the little state of Plataea, in Boeotia, had owed its independence to Athenian protection against its powerful neighbor, Thebes. Now, upon hearing that the feared Persians had come from distant parts to destroy Athens, the Plataeans marched with their entire armed force to assist their benefactors. The small column, perhaps six hundred strong, marching by the southern ridge of Mount Cithaeron, thence across Attica to Marathon, stirred the spirits of the Athenians. It was a brave demonstration, but a few hundred Plataeans were no Spartan army, and the revelation that it would be another six days, at best, before the Spartans turned up must have badly shaken the Athenians.

A council of war was now held in the camp on the hillside. It comprised, according to Herodotus, the ten generals and the polemarch. The generals, then elected annually, enjoyed equal authority. They included Miltiades and Themistocles, whose fortunes have already been outlined, and a soldier-politician of great prospects named Aristides, known to history for his impartiality as "the Just."

The powers of the polemarch at that time have never been well defined. Already the board of generals was encroaching on the old rank of war leader and would soon replace it altogether. Meanwhile, it was something of an anachronism. In 490 B.C., the title was held by Callimachus, an Athenian of noble birth. It may be fair to regard him as the president of a congress of generals. It seems he had a decisive vote in the war council, but did not necessarily command the army in battle. The question of a supreme commander in the field is confused, and Herodotus helps little by being inconsistent, suggesting both that the generals took command in daily rotation and that the polemarch retained his old ascendancy.

At all events, the issue before the council was crystal clear:

should they, or should they not, continue to sit out another week in the hopes of a Spartan arrival?

The options were limited. They could withdraw and hand every advantage to the Persians, or they could accept an engagement on the enemy's terms, that is, on the plain. Characteristically, Miltiades was for fighting. Some of the generals supported him. The rest, perhaps the majority, certainly half the board, were for waiting. They had a strong case. They had checked the invaders now for several days. It was worth being patient a while longer. With the Spartans at their side, a pitched battle would seem a more even risk. As it was, the numerical disparity was too great.

But there was one contingency which might overrule all such caution. If Hippias's agents could use this eerie delay to break the nerves, change the mood of resistance in Athens and spark a coup, then waiting would be tantamount to surrendering the city without a fight.

This, tradition has it, was the argument Miltiades used on the polemarch. "Opinion is divided among the ten of us, some for fighting, some against. Fail to fight, and I see a deterioration of spirit among the Athenians, a division of factions, which will lead to a compact with the enemy. But fight before the rot sets in and, if the gods are willing, we can get the better of them. It therefore rests with you, Callimachus. Support my view, and Athens shall not only be free but the foremost city in Hellas. Support those who decline to fight, and the reverse will become true."

Such, in essence, was the speech of Miltiades as Herodotus conjured it. It must be assumed, of course, that the general based his case on something more substantial than airy rhetoric. He was a forceful advocate, not short of enemies in Athens at whom to point suspicion. Further, his practical knowledge of Persian campaigning gave a certain authority to his optimistic view of a battle with Datis.

True, his dominating and autocratic attitudes, together with his unsavory history, were inimical to democratic philosophy, and the army was full of democrats. But this was no moment for ideological prejudice.

A hostile democracy had preserved Miltiades where a hostile despotism would not have thought twice before destroying him, and if Miltiades now proved correct in his counsel, then Athens might well be rewarded, for Callimachus was persuaded by the argument.

It was decided: provided the sacrificial omens were favorable, the citizens would attack.

The supernatural is abnormally scant in the legend of Marathon, whose embellishments are remarkably worldly—dubious figures and political allusions—for an age which found miracles at least as credible as statistical exaggerations.

Nevertheless, belief in the superhuman was as important in warfare as in the rest of Greek life. The average Greek was as matter-of-fact in his prayers as in his notion of the deities. It was not for any mystic blessing that he begged the gods, but for tangible benefits: rain, prosperity, victory in battle. Nor did he do so shamefacedly. So long as *They* were in a good mood, and he guaranteed an adequate quid pro quo by way of offerings, he saw no reason to be denied satisfaction.

If this view seems oddly at variance with the scientific and philosophic brilliance of ancient Athens, whose intellectual circles included atheists, irreverent playwrights, and certainly many who argued over the nature of the gods and disclaimed their intervention in mundane affairs, it must be remembered that the scientific approach was very new and confined to a small section of society. The majority—indeed the state itself —while pretty tolerant of private nonconformity, adhered staunchly to conventional religious attitudes.

Today, an apprentice metalworker would not expect to recompense heaven for his new skills. But the Athenian apprentice would make an offering to Hephaestus, the god of fire and forges, for his success. A sick Athenian would believe it more important to make a dedication to Asclepius, the god of healing, than to pay a doctor, while a man of outstanding strength and endurance would be supposed to have the help of a benign god.

Superstition was widespread and frequently chronic. Anything from a sneeze to a thunderclap might be construed an omen for good or bad. The gods knew the future and conveyed the message to men in the flight of birds. Skilled interpreters could transcribe it. Or predictions could be obtained from heaven via oracles, soothsayers, even the intestines of a slaughtered sheep.

The belief that the gods are not only all-powerful but all-knowing is not unique to the ancient Greeks, but the confidence with which they reckoned to tap divine knowledge would be difficult to surpass. The significance of such convictions at times of crisis is obvious. Practical considerations might be argued to the last degree, but in the final resort, no prudent man put his plan into action without consulting the signs, and this the Athenians now did at Marathon.

Communal prayers were accompanied by a sacrifice, from which were deduced indications of divine response. The ceremony might be described as a form of field service conducted by an army chaplain. First, an altar was built of turf or rough stones, a fire kindled and the participants sprinkled with water. Then, calling for silence, the priest raised his face to the heavens and prayed loudly for victory. Next, the sacrificial victim —sheep, pig or ox—was led to the altar. To a shout of acclaim from the gathered troops, its throat was cut and the spurt of blood directed into the flame, while a flutist began to play sacred music. The animal was skinned and carved, some fatty bones placed in the fire so the aroma might ascend to the gods, and the rest of the carcass distributed among the communicants. At the same time, prognostications were drawn from the behavior of flames and smoke, and from the constitution of the victim's liver.

Priest and expounders bent to their subtle task. The fire spluttered greasily high above the blue bay. At length, the verdict was announced: the omens were favorable. The warriors began to don their battle garb.

27 "Strike for Freedom!"

Helmets gleaming, crests bristling, the autumnal sun reflecting in their breastplates, the citizens of Athens moved down the hillside in their ten tribes, accompanied by the Plataeans and their commander, Arimnestus. Callimachus, the polemarch, strode ahead of his own tribe, Aeantis. The others followed, picking their footing on the dry slopes, coiling between thickets, smothering goat tracks, surging and jostling in their bronzed regiments: Erechtheis, Aegis, Pandionis, Leontis, Acamantis, Oeneis, Cecropis, Hippothontis, Antiochis.

The hills abounded in powerful and exemplary fable. Marathon, as a region, was sacred to Heracles, son of Zeus and the most illustrious hero in Greek myth, renowned for his manly strength. Nearby was the spring of Macaria, his daughter, who had sacrificed herself for the liberty of her kin. The very plain on which the battle would rage was the scene of many stories about Theseus, hero of Athens. Here, too, so legend told, the Athenians, with the descendants of Heracles, the Heraclidae, had routed the invader Eurystheus, king of Mycenae. In the minds of those now descending to the battlefield, these were no idle fictions, but, for most, matters of earnest faith and urgent emulation. Those superbeings who once had struggled and suffered on the same spot could scarcely look down now without sympathy.

At the same time, the Athenians would not have been Greeks had they failed to face up to practicalities. For Miltiades especially, the prospects must have nagged with grim subtlety. Experience with both types of army gave an educated edge to his anticipation. He knew how the Persians would expect to fight. The salient features of Persian warfare were the skilled deployment of bowmen, skirmishers and cavalry. They used speed and maneuverability to outflank and harry the enemy, while bowmen disorganized his ranks with their crippling arrow flights. Persian archery was alarmingly accurate, and lethal at up to perhaps a hundred and twenty yards. In rout and pursuit, their cavalry and fleet spearmen were merciless.

By contrast, the Athenians, in common with other Greeks, were trained to fight in a tight and ponderous phalanx, depending on their traditional Hellenic foes to do likewise. Like lumbering rhinos, they charged head-on. The Greek phalanx of the period was normally of eight ranks, each line abreast and tight on the heels of the one in front. Its hoplite rankers were shoulder to shoulder, probably occupying little more than three square feet apiece in a formation whose effectiveness depended largely on its weight and cohesion. To gain advantage on impact, some Greek armies charged at the double, though only over the last few score paces, since running in armor was exhausting and the phalanx tended to disintegrate when moving quickly. Indeed, the most renowned of Greek warriors, the Spartans, preferred to advance slowly right up to the enemy, relying on the perfection and density of their formation to absorb his onslaught.

Greek generals had a dread of being outnumbered. Where humanly possible, the Hellenic states avoided combat unless their armies were numerically on a par with the enemy. Their commanders also lived in fear of the flank attack, to which they were unaccustomed and vulnerable. Against this, Miltiades doubtless gambled the superiority of the armored hoplite to the Persian warrior at close quarters—assuming the Athenians could get to close quarters through the customary hail of Persian arrows.

From a detached point of view, the profound difference in the evolution of Greek and Persian warfare promised an absorbing battle of wit and resolution. But battles are not fought in the mood of detachment, and the most cerebral of the

Athenian citizens thronging to the plain at Marathon is unlikely to have relished the intellectual exercise. The distant swarm spreading from the Persian camp, its outriders probably marked by trailing dust plumes, was composed not of pawns in some tidy textbook theory, but of alien flesh and blood to be grappled, pierced and smashed with brute fury if the Greeks themselves were not to perish, their city to become a slave depot for the Orient.

On reaching the edge of the plain, the Athenians arrayed themselves in their preordained phalanx. As was customary, the polemarch commanded the right wing, presumably backed by the ranks of his own tribe, while the Plataeans now formed on the far left. In the center, the Leontis and Antiochis regiments stood side by side, with Themistocles and Aristides in prominence.

The position of Miltiades remains obscure. According to Herodotus, the attack took place on a day when, under the alleged scheme of rotating command, Miltiades held precedence. But, in any case, the scribe says, the generals supporting his strategy had agreed to give up their turns to him. Even so, it is not clear that he supplanted the supremacy of the polemarch during the engagement.

To some extent, the question of overall command of the army in actual battle was less important than later concepts of military action have led analysts to suppose. Dispositions and simple orders were announced in advance, and everyone knew his place in the phalanx. Variations on the conventional set-piece action were not expected in Greek warfare until one side was beaten, when individual captains probably resorted to their own initiative.

Though the confrontation at Marathon was unconventional, the Athenians seemingly adhered to traditional methods, with the exception of a few tactical innovations. These certainly suggest the influence of Miltiades to the extent that they anticipated special dangers inherent in tackling the Persians.

But they might well have been authorized by Callimachus or agreed on in council by the board of generals.

The first was the lateral extension of the phalanx to prevent the Persians from outflanking the Greek wings. Had they drawn up in the normal eight-rank formation, facing roughly north up the plain toward the Charadra stream, the Athenians would have covered rather less than half the front between the rising ground on their left and the sea on their right. Instead, the number of ranks in the central section was reduced to give extra breadth, while the wings retained their full depth. By reducing the depth of the phalanx in part to, say, four ranks, it could be stretched considerably—not to span the plain entirely (the distance between the sea and the inland heights was almost two miles)—but at least to cramp the space beyond the extremities of the formation. Just conceivably, this adjustment was carried out as the phalanx advanced. Far more likely, it was devised and implemented at the outset.

As the citizens took station at the plain's edge, the enemy was about a mile ahead, in front of the Charadra, and deploying rapidly. Datis would have been warned by his lookouts as soon as the Greek army broke camp, and it did not take the lightly equipped Persians long to grab bows and spears, and slip bridles on their horses. Nevertheless, the eastern general cannot have had as much time as he would have liked to extend his myriads, nor could there have been many minutes in hand once the Athenians started forward across the plain.

Doubtless, Datis regretted the low strength of his cavalry at Marathon, compared with the great force of horsemen the Iranians liked to use for fast maneuvering. But there was little time for pondering the ideal. Suddenly, to the south of the teeming Asians, a defiant roar proclaimed the advance of the Athenians. The dilated phalanx heaved and flexed as the hoplites swung ahead in their gilded ranks.

Aeschylus, now striding in station with his countrymen, recalled in his *Persae* the exhortations which spurred the

Greeks in their conflicts with the Persians: "On, sons of Hellas! Strike for the freedom of your land! Strike for the liberty of your children and of your wives; for the shrines of the ancestral gods and the tombs of your fathers! All are staked on the contest." And no doubt, there were coarser, less literary rumblings.

To the front, in the finest of helms and corselets, stomped the leaders, holding the line in steady order. Behind them, youth and age—boyish fear and seasoned apprehension—united in the swagger of an armored front, came the manhood of Athens, rich and poor, intellectual and artisan, scrawny and corpulent—nine thousand part-time soldiers to stem the vanguard of the universal eastern despot. Herodotus says that when the Persians saw the Greeks advancing, "without horse or bowmen, and scanty in numbers, they thought them a set of madmen bent on certain destruction."

Be that as it may, Datis must have wondered at the novelty of the sight. Never before had a Persian general faced an attacking Greek phalanx, and the unexpectedness of those slow-moving lines of footmen, approaching as if on a country walk, may well have provoked changes in his contingency planning.

The vulnerable center of the formation, strung long and thin across the grassy flats, was an inviting target. There is some evidence that the conquering Mede was tempted to adopt an unusually static disposition in the conviction that he could shred the attenuated Greek line with arrow-fire, then overwhelm it by sheer concentration of numbers. Certainly, the Persians faced the center of the phalanx in heavy mass.

The gap was narrowing between the armies. At perhaps a quarter of a mile, the Persian bowmen plucked their first arrows and eyed the unbroken wall of plodding hoplites with professional confidence. Bronze helmet and breastplate might afford some protection from the missiles, but there were plenty of soft marks, and the trundling phalanx would be very hard to miss when it came into bowshot.

At two hundred yards, the archers began to flex their weapons. The ripple and flux of the Greek line, well over a mile long, must have called for constant adjustments of pace in the regiments to maintain its dressing. The squall of abuse and taunts from the two sides would swell as the distance closed. Then, while the archers aimed a lofted volley to fall at perhaps rather more than a hundred yards, the Athenians abruptly leveled their spears and the entire phalanx broke into a loping charge.

Greek tradition avers that the phalanx advanced for eight stades—that is, the full mile from its point of assembly—at the double. This must be treated as the distortion of a memorable tactic. Few citizens could have run a mile and still fought effectively, even assuming the formation could have withstood the excessive strain. Moreover, the Persian bowmen could have adjusted their trajectory to a consistent pace, whereas it is clear that very few arrows found a billet.

Only a sudden acceleration could have baffled them, the first volley overshooting as the Greeks surged forward. It was an auspicious stratagem, later adopted by the Hellenes as a standard ploy against archers. What bowman, save one of suicidal resolution, would have risked a second shot instead of drawing his sidearms?

28 Deadly Toil

Shields high, spears bristling, the Athenian line met the enemy, and so commenced the first of three distinct phases in the battle of Marathon. Carried forward by the impetus of the charge, the citizens smashed into the myriads of Datis, into the "invincible" conquerors.

"Until that day," exclaimed Herodotus, "the very name of the Medes [he used the term to describe both Medes and Persians] struck terror in the ears of the Hellenes." Now, jowl to jowl with the foreigner, there can have been no time for terror—only the primitive bid to destroy and to survive the fray.

Dense as they were, the Persian war gangs must have shuddered at the impact of the phalanx, recoiling abruptly until sheer numbers, and the dead weight of the first casualties, buffered its momentum. The eastern nobles, rallying their warriors, countered Greek spear with scimitar, or Syrian khepesh, and possibly the war-ax as fashioned by Egyptian slave craftsmen.

At closest quarters, the spear could become an embarrassment, liable to be wrested from the grip or inextricably impaled in an enemy. The Greeks unsheathed their broad-bladed swords and hacked at the opposition savagely. The Spartans were the celebrated exponents of close fighting, but now the Athenians outshone the absent westerners for inspiration.

Part-time soldiers the Athenians might be, but they were hard—for the most part fit men, of a race that placed physical prowess at a premium. Many, indeed, were accomplished athletes. Philippides the runner, returned from Sparta, was there in the phalanx wielding a burnished blade. Themistocles and

Aristides, though firstly politicians and diplomats, were accomplished soldiers. Even a poet such as Aeschylus could handle weapons usefully, and was, in fact, to be remembered on his grave as a warrior, not as a tragedian.

These men of Athens, whether artists or adventurers, had imbibed the lives of the heroes from infancy, had anticipated the moment of truth in the sagas. "And close the deadly toil was pitched . . . And thus the black blood flowed on earth . . ." So Homer had pictured the carnage of the Trojan wars; so the citizens found the reality at Marathon. And as the blood flowed, the initial geometry of the ranks contorted in the melting pot of savage force.

Recovered from the Greek charge, the Persian army responded vigorously, checking the lighter files at the center of the phalanx, struggling to stem the weightier Greek wings. Greatly outnumbered, the Leontis, Antiochis and other Athenian regiments of the middle station, were forced back as the Iranian warriors, emulating their zealous dekarchs, rushed in small bands to join the tide threatening to overwhelm the Greek front. The phalanx sagged, but as yet, did not disintegrate.

"The whole line fought valiantly," wrote the ancient scribe. It was the valor of those who have all to lose: homes, families, holy shrines. But it was more than that. It was also the valor of those fighting for a communal ideal; the resolution of a young, politically conscious society whose members had come to enjoy equality and liberty under laws of their own choice, and who now staked everything for their freedom. Herodotus himself acknowledged the force of ideology. "Liberty and equality," he wrote, "are brave, spirit-stirring things."

Not that the Persians were lacking in ideals. They had many —from the ideal of truthfulness to that of a religion in some ways more sublime than the Greek faith. But they were not fighting for such things at Marathon. Warlike as they were, loyal as they might be, dutifully as their nobles approached the field, in the final analysis they were there simply because the king had ordered the humbling of Athens.

And what the king ordered was obeyed without question. Persian law, as the judges of that nation once testified, allowed the monarch to do exactly as he liked.

Great or lowly, the emperor's subjects were as bound by his will as were his hunting dogs. Men, however, lack the canine inclination to be subservient. They may recognize, but they seldom adore absolute authority. They may learn to live with despotism and it may even profit some, but as a cause for which to die, it lacks conviction. Of all the factors favoring Athens at Marathon, it is hard not to conclude that the moral one was the most vital.

Next, perhaps, was the factor of armaments. With the Persian archers neutralized, Datis had lost his ace. At close range the weapons of the average Iranian were inferior to those of the hoplite. The Persian spear was shorter than the Greek spear, the Persian dagger less effective than the Greek sword. The last, even by the times represented in the *Iliad*, was a deadly reaper of opponents' limbs—"many downright hewed from off their shoulders as they fought." Linked with the defensive armor of the Athenians, these factors were now grimly balanced against the numbers of the enemy.

From the slopes of Kotroni and Stavrokoraki, where a few awed peasants may have watched the engagement, the bronze-clad citizens must have glowed like amber insects beleaguered by an army of soldier ants. Tortuously, the thin body of the Greek center was torn apart from the wings, to shrink before the horde of Persians assailing it. With dogged reluctance, Aristides and his fellows retreated, parrying tirelessly.

By contrast, the extremities of the phalanx, isolated but fighting in full depth, not only rammed back the footmen opposed to them, but repulsed whatever harassment came from the cavalry. Probably (the latter is not explicit in tradition), it did not amount to much. Cavalry of the day—indeed, until comparatively modern times—was not given to charging into unbroken foot formations. Instead, the riders spurred close, hurled javelins, then wheeled away. Such tactics were useless once their own infantry came to grips with the enemy, when horsemen could only stand off and await developments.

A mile or more apart, Arimnestus and Callimachus plied their swords relentlessly, urging their eight-deep regiments into the staggering Persian wings. Bull-like, the twin companies—Plataeans to the left, the polemarch's men on the right, away toward the smooth bay—bored forward until their adversaries reeled and ran for safety. It must have been a unique experience for Datis to see his soldiers in headlong flight. At the same time, his central forces, perhaps as numerous as the entire Athenian army, were surging forward, threatening to swamp the Greek line withdrawing ahead of them. Arimnestus and the polemarch acted with alacrity. "When they had gained the upper hand," claimed Herodotus, "they allowed the beaten units of the barbarians to escape, turning inwards themselves to engage those who had driven back the Athenian center."

With the victorious Greek wings converging across the havoc-strewn plain to the relief of their comrades, it may be said that the first phase of the battle had ended and the second was commencing.

Lofted above the heaving shoulders and glinting weapons of their thronging warriors, the Persian captains—mounted, mailed and helmeted—must have noted apprehensively the transformation of dispositions. For many thousands of their men to be engaged to the front, and assaulted on both flanks simultaneously, was an ironic and dangerous reversal of the situation normally contrived by the Iranians.

That the second stage of Marathon was frantic and sanguinary in the extreme is beyond doubt. In the powerful breast of the Asian force, bands of blooded tribesmen, deprived of their kill at the point of triumph, turned furiously against the flanking Athenians.

The Greek phalanx was no longer an entity. Its center,

though now relieved of some pressure, had suffered a cruel ordeal. Nor can the wing regiments, if still strong, have retained the immaculate ranks of later theory as they hustled, already sore and blown, to the rescue. More likely, they fought in rugged bands, tightly clustered—trousered Persian and skirted Greek locked in swirling scrimmages.

Centuries later, the Greek travel writer Pausanias described a painting of the combat he saw on a portico in the market at Athens. High above the melee, the artist had depicted the gods and goddesses in phantom audience. "Of the combatants," wrote Pausanias, "the most conspicuous are Callimachus, the Athenian war leader; Miltiades, one of the generals; and a hero called Echetlus."

Echetlus seems to have been one of those fabulous figures, part real perhaps, part fantasy, who not infrequently grow from the trauma of battle into national consciousness. Born in military reminiscence as an anonymous peasant who appeared in the thick of the fracas wielding a plowshare against the foe, he acquired a name and a place among the heroes as time passed.

Another battle story told of a certain Epizelus, who was struck blind in the conflict. The last vision, it appears, of this ill-fated citizen, was of a monstrous bearded easterner striking down the blinded man's neighbor.

With more certainty, one can imagine the high-crested and aggressive Miltiades thundering execrations as he hacked at the enemy. Or a brawny Cynaegirus, noted for his boldness, cleaving a gory path.

"Long time the battle raged," according to the old account. But since the disorganized wings of the Persian army, though not pursued, apparently failed to reinforce the center, it seems reasonable to suppose the bloody struggle there was a quick one. In something like equal numbers, the Athenians were masters of the Asians.

Supporting their wounded, the invaders fell back on the line of ships. The mounds of dead they abandoned grimly evidenced the Persian error in allowing the Greeks to fight on their own terms, at close quarters. Wicker shields were no protection against the chopping blades of the hoplites, nor were ferocity and agility enough in themselves to break the bronze walls of the Greek shields.

For the first time in his career, Datis faced the prospect of defeat. Whether, at this stage, he personally conceded Marathon is irrelevant. The decision was made for him. Men conditioned to winning easily, as had the Persians at every stage of their advance from Samos, are not well prepared to turn a losing fight, to snatch victory from disaster.

Nothing remained but to salvage the day by an effective reembarkation. With this operation, and the accompanying rearguard action, the conflict enters its final phase.

In Greek tradition, the Persian retreat was a total rout. "Then they [the Athenians] pursued the flying Persians and cut them down till they reached the sea," proclaimed Herodotus. "And they called for fire and began to attack the ships." Of the artist's impression in the portico at Athens, Pausanias reported: "At the extremity of the picture are the Phoenician ships and the Greeks slaughtering the barbarians who are rushing to board them." Fleeing Persians were depicted pushing each other into the marsh at the plain's end.

Yet the ancient evidence is contradictory. Herodotus makes an exceptional point of Greek losses in the battle for the beaches, including two of particular significance. "In this part of the conflict, the polemarch Callimachus lost his life after fighting gallantly, and general Stesilaus, son of Thrasylaus, was slain. Here Cynaegirus, son of Euphorion, had his hand lopped off by an axe while grappling the stern of a vessel, and fell, as did many other Athenians of note." At no other stage of the fight is reference made to the loss of high-ranking commanders. It is as if there was a need for special leadership against this alleged rout. In fact, the inescapable inference, not of a rout but of a stiff rearguard action, is reinforced by further information that the bulk of the invasion force reembarked success-fully, a mere seven vessels falling to the pursuing Greeks.

It has been suggested that after the defeat of the Persian center, the exhausted citizens of Athens and their Plataean allies paused to rest and collect themselves. One can plausibly elaborate the theory. It may well be that the prospect of a further attack on Datis's army, reunited in the area of the fleet, daunted even the triumphant but weary Greeks. In which case, rather than pressing a so-far kindly providence, it is possible they allowed part of the Persian army to embark unmolested before launching the ultimate onslaught.

At all events, the indications suggest a hectic tussle. In the fate of Cynaegirus is hinted a desperate tug of war, the Athenians clinging to the sterns of the galleys to prevent their departure, oarsmen threshing in the shallows, while drenched warriors dueled in the breakers at the water's edge.

When at last the triremes had pulled beyond danger, the Greeks could take stock of the day's work. Of the maimed and critically injured there is no record, nor were the Plataean casualties mentioned. For the rest, the Athenian losses were put at 192 dead, the Persians killed at an extraordinary 6,400. There seems no reason to doubt the first figure, for the slain were buried on the battlefield and the names of the Greeks inscribed on ten tribal columns which marked the spot. Though now lost, the columns stood to be consulted for a long time. And, if the number of seriously wounded is reckoned at rather more than the dead, then one militiaman in twenty paid dearly for the victory.

The figure for Persians killed—a Greek claim; there are no counterstatistics—is less believable. Few, if any, nations fail to magnify the losses they inflict on their enemies, and there is no cause to exempt the Athenians. A ratio of more than thirty slaughtered Asians for every dead Greek seems beyond the disparity in morale and armaments, and should probably be related to the generally exaggerated views concerning the Persian force. All the same, the invaders must have suffered severely to have swallowed the pride of generations of imperial glory and retreated from the army of a reputedly petty state.

And retreat they had, with unequivocal urgency, leaving behind not only their dead but the rich treasure and equipage of their beachhead encampment. The Athenians turned it to gracious use. From the proceeds they built a marble shrine in honor of the gods, at Delphi, the holiest place in Greece, decorating it with a representation of the deities battling with the giants—a fitting tribute from a people who had, themselves, proved to be giant killers.

Meanwhile, on the evening of the struggle, Athens was still not entirely safe. To the discomfort of the conquering citizens at Marathon, the retiring galleys did not stand out for southern Euboea and the eastern roads, but made south down the coast toward Cape Sunium. The implications were ominous.

Datis had seen enough of the Athenian army. The plan for establishing a tyrant in the state could be forgotten. Yet total failure, and the ignominy, even danger, of reporting it to Darius, might still be averted. By bearing west around the southern cape and putting in to the bay of Phalerum, it was possible the Persians could sack the adjacent city of Athens before its soldiers had marched home from Marathon. It was a rancorous plan, but then Datis and his cohorts were hardly in a honeyed mood, and from the first the theme of the expedition was retribution.

The destructive capability of the eastern army was still high. Even granting the Persian losses based on tradition, it could still land thousands of able-bodied warriors, more than enough to overrun a near-defenseless Athens and very quickly render it in ruins.

An incident surrounded by some mystery was reported to have occurred as the Persians left Marathon. A sun signal, it was said, was flashed by shield from one of the inland heights to the battlefield. This was interpreted popularly by a later generation as advice from conspirators in Athens that they were prepared to receive the invaders. If so—and the signalers were clearly unaware of the battle and its outcome—the destruction of the city might actually be facilitated from the inside. One way or another, the Athenian generals had to move fast. Leaving a contingent to tend the wounded, they assembled the fit men and set off, marching from the precinct, or holy compound, of Heracles at Marathon to a precinct of Heracles close to Athens. The connection perhaps appealed to the impressionable citizens. It was a long tramp for muscles chilled in the open hills and stiffened on the battlefield, but the ranks were in good heart and the necessity urgent.

The effort crowned their accomplishment. Though Datis lingered awhile off Phalerum contemplating the temple-capped Acropolis, the only signal now from the shore was the twinkling armor of the hoplites, an invitation he had no intention of accepting a second time.

Twice confounded, the Persians steered for Asia.

Postscript

Approaching the plain of Marathon by the coast road from Athens, Mount Agrieliki is on the left; the bay, stretching away to its northern promontory, on the right. Today, dwellings, crops and olive groves adorn the battlefield, but the Soros, or burial mound of the fallen Athenians, can still be seen by the traveler. It lies roughly halfway between the foot of Agrieliki and the Charadra, and nearer the sea than the inland heights.

Pausanias, who found the memorial columns still standing six centuries after the battle, believed the place to be haunted. "Here every night," he wrote, "you may hear horses neighing and men fighting. To go on purpose to see the sight brought good to no man, but the spirits are not angered by he who lights on it by accident."

Legend waxed swiftly on the epic confrontation. Gods and supermen had battled for Athens; phantom champions dispensed their timeless skills among the citizens. Pan had struck terror in the Persians; divine will turned aside their arrows. Fables of a worldlier kind became as prominent. Athenian militiamen had performed feats of prodigious energy and endurance; the retreat of the Greek center had been a brilliantly calculated maneuver to lure the enemy to his doom; Miltiades had both planned and led the execution of the victory.

The impulses to embroider and transfigure are not hard to elucidate. Firstly there was the Greek addiction to the marvelous—already under question by the post-Marathonian period, but still a potent force for long to come. Secondly, there was the vanity of the Athenians. Thirdly, there was the determination of the family and adherents of Miltiades to exalt his services, and the exploitation of his prestige by opponents of the democrats.

Unfortunately, there was no historian at Marathon to bequeath an eyewitness record of what happened. It was not until Herodotus reached maturity, with the next generation, that posterity was blessed with a brief, and though truly invaluable, inevitably frustrating account of the battle. Since references to the campaign by other ancient writers add little of a trustworthy nature, it is not surprising that subsequent interpretations have been as varied as they have been ingenious, and that little can be asserted which is not frankly speculative.

Conflicting theories have been proposed to cover every aspect of Marathon. (For the purposes of the foregoing reconstruction, let it be declared that Herodotus has been supplemented by a general study of ancient warfare, and tempered at the unfashionable, but still functional, wayside forge of common sense.) It has been argued that the Persians drew the Greeks to Marathon as a deliberate preliminary to a sea attack on Athens; that part of the Persian army had already embarked before the Greeks charged; that the Athenians were on their way to Eretria when the invaders landed; that the phalanx advanced from the east, not the south; that the Persians fought with their backs to the sea, not to the Charadra; and that a score more different assumptions are the correct ones.

Many of these theories are intriguing, some are amusing in that they virtually dismiss Herodotus, the one historian who lived within living memory of the event, and none, beyond a miracle, can ever be disproved. Even the year of the battle is disputed in some circles, let alone the actual day of the lunar month.

It seems that the Spartans, in accord with their promise, set out on the morning following the full moon, having perhaps already assembled on their near border, for they are said to have joined the Athenians after a march of only three days: that is, late on the eighteenth—fixing the fight within the preceding two or three days. Too late to help, but curious to view the Persian corpses, the Spartans visited the battlefield, where their professional admiration soared for the hitherto unadmired

Athenians. Indeed, one of the primary consequences of Marathon was the enormous prestige it gave Athens throughout Greece, and the confidence it bestowed on Athenian democracy.

The fortunes of Miltiades soon waned. Shortly after the Persian departure, his fellow-citizens granted him, on his own proposal, a naval commission in the Cyclades, where loyalties had been thrown into some doubt by the activities of the armada. Commanding a fleet of galleys, he landed on Paros and laid siege to its city, ostensibly to punish the Parians for furnishing Datis with a trireme. Eventually, having failed to breach the island's defenses, Miltiades returned to Athens wounded, where he was accused before a popular tribunal of criminally deceiving the people and sentenced to a heavy fine. The character of the deception is now obscure. According to legend, he had persuaded the assembly to entrust him with the fleet on the promise of leading it to a rich source of gold but attacked Paros instead to gratify a private grudge.

At Paros, the tale was preserved that he had corrupted a priestess named Timo in the temple of Demeter, outside the city, and received his injury fleeing after an assignation in a sanctuary reserved for women. Whatever the circumstances, the damage must have been serious. Miltiades appeared on a couch at his trial, and died not long afterward.

The fate of the Persian commanders is unknown. Doubtless, their report to the emperor minimized the failure in Attica while stressing the successes at Naxos, Carystus, Eretria and elsewhere. Darius might have fumed at his second sting from Athens, but can only have regarded it as a temporary check. It did, however, have awkward repercussions in the empire. The defeat of a Persian army was not the sort of news easily hushed up, and in Egypt, burdened with its share of war taxes, it stirred the embers of latent disaffection to sudden flame. In 486 B.C., a certain Khabisha, proclaiming relationship to Psammeticus, was hailed as Pharaoh.

Darius prepared his strategies unhurriedly. There can have

been little doubt in his mind of the outcome. Egypt, which had prospered considerably through his rule, would be brought to order with a firm hand, and those Greeks who continued to mar his western horizon would be subordinated to the world's greatest governing complex. Two armies were assembled to tackle the projects, but Darius never issued their marching orders. Instead came the stunning information that the king was dead. He had reigned for thirty-five years, and time was no heeder of emperors.

A few miles north of his winter palace at Persepolis the great despot was interred in a tomb hewed from solid rock. Beside the entrance were carved four pillars bearing the heads of bulls, above which a façade depicting the subject peoples of Persia was topped by an image of the dead monarch, bow in hand, and the winged symbol of Mazda. An inscribed panegyric recounted the accomplishments of Darius—in the words of Darius. So pass the omnipotent.

While no battle can have had a greater impact on history than that of Marathon, it did not, for long, settle anything. Social evolution does not depend on proximate causes.

Momentarily, by thwarting the immediate objectives of Darius, the Athenians had averted disaster. But the inevitability of collision between Greece and an expanding Persian empire rested on a law more inexorable than that of any passing argument between governments, and could not have been halted whatever the outcome of a single fight. What Darius had started, others would have to continue. Marathon was not the end of a war, merely the prologue to a series of bigger battles—Artemisium, Salamis, Plataea, the Eurymedon—in which Greece finally united in awareness of its collective peril.

The wider importance of that first clash in Attica was that by breaking the paralyzing spell of Persian invincibility, it inspirited Greece to withstand the empire, and ultimately to triumph, rather than to submit piecemeal as might otherwise have happened. It is unnecessary to contemplate hordes of oriental warriors overrunning Europe upon the hypothetical fall of Greece in order to emphasize the magnitude of Marathon. It is a moot point whether, had they conquered the Balkans, the Iranians would have gone on (as some have suggested) to forestall the Roman empire. But quite positively, in the suppositional circumstances, that empire could not have been the product of the Rome known to history, for the culture of Rome was, of course, inherited from Greece.

If Marathon saved Greece (at least, the ancient Greece known to posterity), then the militiamen of Callimachus preserved the essence of western civilization, which first developed in Greek society. And if today's despots are small fry—political rivalry largely centered on the economic systems of popular governments—that, too, owes something to Marathon. But such allusions, if teasing, are not of this story.

The Athenians themselves never lost sight of Marathon, looking back on the day as the outset of an epoch. Attica abounded in memorials of the conflict. Pausanias described a huge statue of the goddess Nemesis carved out of a block of marble which, legend told, had been provided by Datis to form a trophy of his anticipated victory. As Nemesis had once indulged her taste for dramatic reverses upon the opulent Croesus, so, it pleased the Athenians to postulate, had she sported with the Persians at Marathon. The statue was placed in a temple to the goddess at Rhamnus, about eight miles from the battlefield. Athens preserved many reminders of the great day, including the pictures on the painted porch and a sculptured image of the battle on the Temple of Victory, on the Acropolis. Along with other tributes, these appeared several decades after the conflict, for it was not only by the generation of that time that the importance of Marathon was recognized.

At the height of its intellectual splendor and prosperity, through the long autumn of its decline and for centuries beyond its eventual fall, Athens recalled Marathon as its finest hour. Periodically, religious services were held to honor the fallen, while politicians quickly learned the emotive force of a plea to the memory of those heroes.

"Nothing," wrote one historian, "was omitted that could keep alive the remembrance of a deed which had first taught the Athenian people to know its own strength by measuring it with the power which had subdued the greater part of the known world. The consciousness thus awakened fixed its character, its station, and its destiny."

It was as if, that day, the gods had sanctified freedom.

Forgivably, perhaps, the last lines of this tale have been reserved for its first performer, the runner Philippides.

When the battle was done, so the story goes, Philippides was called from the ranks of exhausted citizens and entrusted to carry the brave news to Athens. Once more, the enduring athlete faced the stony road, this time a comparative trifle of twenty-two miles, spurred by the brilliance of his tidings.

It is this exploit—the run from the scene of travail through the mountains to the prayerful city—which is commemorated in the "marathon" road race of the modern Olympic games, while the greater but unproductive run to Sparta has lacked celebration.

But the exertions of the battle, on top of his haul to Laconia, had enfeebled even Philippides, and though euphoria bore him irrepressibly onward, he was spent when he drew in sight of the conurbation. Legend tells how he staggered through the city gates, uttered a single exultant cry, and collapsed, dying. With Robert Browning, we may conclude on a romantic note:

> He saw the land saved he had helped to save, and was suffered to tell
> Such tidings, yet never decline, but, gloriously as he began,
> So to end gloriously—once to shout, thereafter be mute:
> "Athens is saved!"

Selected Bibliography

Since this is a storybook and not a tome for scholars, a compilation of sources, primary and general, would be as pretentious as it would be extensive. Instead, I have tried to pick out a few English-language volumes and shorter studies on a variety of topics raised (the titles are self-explanatory) with a view to providing some onward interest for the tenderfoot who might care to explore one or another trail.

Adcock, F.E. *The Greek and Macedonian Art of War.* (Sather Lectures XXX) Berkeley and Los Angeles, 1957.

Andrewes, A. *The Greeks.* London, 1967.

Bury, J.B. *History of Greece to the Death of Alexander the Great.* London, 1931.

Cameron, G. *Early History of Iran.* Chicago, 1936.

Carnoy, A.J. *Iranian Mythology.* London, 1917.

Clay, A.T. "Gobryas, Governor of Babylonia," *Journal American Oriental Society,* XLI, 1922.

Cook, R.M. *Greek Painted Pottery.* London, 1960.

Curzon, G.N. *Persia.* London, 1892.

Davison, J.A. "The First Greek Triremes," *Classical Quarterly,* XLI, 1947.

Devambez, P. *Greek Painting.* London, 1962.

Dunham, A.G. *History of Miletus.* London, 1915.

Ehrenberg, V. *The People of Aristophanes.* London, 1951.

French, A. *The Growth of the Athenian Economy.* London, 1964.

Frye, Richard N. *The Heritage of Persia.* London, 1962.

Gardiner, E.N. *Athletics of the Ancient World.* Oxford, 1930.

Gershevitch, I. "Iranian Literature," in E. B. Ceadel (ed.), *Literatures of the East.* London, 1953.

Gomme, A.W. *Essays in Greek History and Literature.* Oxford, 1937.

Guthrie, W.K.C. *The Greeks and Their Gods.* London, 1950.

Hammond, N.G.L. *History of Greece to 322 B.C.* Oxford, 1959.

Hignett, C. *History of the Athenian Constitution.* Oxford, 1952.

How, W.W. "Cornelius Nepos on Marathon and Paros," *Journal of Hellenic Studies,* XXXIX, 1919.

210   ALAN LLOYD

————. Arms, Tactics and Strategy in the Persian Wars. *Journal of Hellenic Studies*, XLIII, 1923.

James, H.R. *Our Hellenic Heritage*, Vol I. London, 1921.

Jones, A.H.M. *Athenian Democracy*. London, 1957.

Lesky, A. *History of Greek Literature*. London, 1966.

Levy, R. *Persian Literature*. London, 1923.

Livingstone, R.W. (ed) *The Legacy of Greece*. Oxford, 1922.

Mackenzie, Compton. *Marathon and Salamis*. London, 1934.

Minns, E.H. *Scythians and Greeks*. Cambridge, 1913.

Moulton, J.H. *Early Religious Poetry of Persia*. Cambridge, 1911.

Munro, J.A.R. "Some Observations on the Persian Wars," *Journal of Hellenic Studies*, XIX, 1899.

Myres, J.L. *Herodotus: Father of History*. Oxford, 1953.

Nilsson, M.P. *Greek Piety*. Oxford, 1948.

Olmstead, A.T. *History of the Persian Empire*. Chicago, 1948.

Parke, H.W. *Greek Oracles*. London, 1967.

Powell, J.E. *The History of Herodotus*. Cambridge, 1939.

————. *Herodotus* (translation). Oxford, 1949.

Richter, G.M.A. *Handbook of Greek Art*. London, 1959.

Rogers, R.W. *History of Ancient Persia*. London and New York, 1929.

Rose, H.J. *Handbook of Greek Mythology*. London, 1964.

Rostovtzeff, M. *Iranians and Greeks in Southern Russia*. Oxford, 1922.

Schwab, Gustav. *Gods and Heroes, Myths and Epics of Ancient Greece*. New York, 1946; London, 1947.

Seltman, Charles. *Women in Antiquity*. London, 1956.

Sykes, Sir P. *History of Persia*, Vol I. London, 1930.

Tarn, W.W. *Hellenistic Military and Naval Developments*. Cambridge, 1930.

Tucker, T.G. *Life in Ancient Athens*. London, 1912.

Wardman, A.E. "Tactics and the Tradition of the Persian Wars," *Historia*, VIII, 1959.

Webster, T.B.L. *Everyday Life in Classical Athens*. London and New York, 1969.

Wilson, R.D. "Darius the Mede," *Princeton Theological Review*, 1922.

Wycherly, R.E. *How the Greeks Built Cities*. London, 1949.

Zachner, R.C. *The Dawn and Twilight of Zoroastrianism*. London, 1961.

About the Author

ALAN LLOYD is a distinguished and successful writer of books of popular history. Among his books are *The Spanish Centuries, The Making of the King 1066, The Last of the Impis, The Drums of Kumasi, The Maligned Monarch, The King Who Lost America* and *Franco.* He lives in Kent, England, with his family.